WRITING
HOME

Cindy La Ferle 2005 (handwritten signature)

CINDY LA FERLE

—

WRITING

HOME

—

Collected essays and

newspaper columns

from 1992 - 2004

Hearth Stone Books
Royal Oak, Michigan

The author owns all rights to the essays and columns in this collection, but wishes to acknowledge the following magazines and newspapers in which some of the pieces previously appeared:

Better Homes & Gardens: Country Gardens Magazine
The Christian Science Monitor
The Daily Tribune (Royal Oak, Michigan)
The Daily Oakland Press (Pontiac, Michigan)
The Detroit Free Press
Healing Garden Journal
The Mirror of Royal Oak
Mary Engelbreit's Home Companion
Reader's Digest
Traverse City Record Eagle
Unity Magazine

Anthologies
09/11: 8:48 a.m.: Documenting America's Greatest Tragedy,
edited by BlueEar.com: Global Writing Worth Reading
A Century of Voices: An Anthology of Detroit Women Writers,
edited by Corinne Abatt et al

Cover design: Douglas La Ferle
Author photo: Rick Smith

Hearth Stone Books is an imprint of Self-Reliance Press.
For more information address Hearth Stone Books, 1525
Vinsetta Blvd., Royal Oak, MI 48067
first edition

Library of Congress Cataloging-in-Publication Data

La Ferle, Cindy, 1954-
Writing home / Cindy La Ferle.
p. cm.
ISBN 0-923568-63-8
1. Motherhood—Michigan—Anecdotes. 2. Michigan—Social life and customs—Anecdotes. I. Title.
HQ759.L2 2005
306.874'3—dc22
2004025196

Manufactured in the United States of America

To Doug La Ferle, Nate La Ferle, and Carlesta Gullion;
and in loving memory of William Gullion.
Thank you for being my family,
the story of my life.

To all my "Shrine kids" and to my Soul Sisters.
Thank you for opening your doors and your hearts
and extending my family circle.

I long, as does every human being,
to be home wherever I find myself.

—Maya Angelou

Contents

Preface

At a writers' retreat I attended several years ago, author Madeleine L'Engle posed the question, "Why do all of us want to share our stories?" Her answer affirmed what each of us knew but couldn't express quite as elegantly: "We share our stories because we have faith—faith that the universe has meaning, and that our little lives are not irrelevant."

After working as a travel editor in the late 1980s, I began writing short essays and book reviews—an unexpected career detour that led to part-time work writing personal columns for magazines and newspapers. While it didn't draw much of an income, I still believe it was the best assignment I've ever had. For one thing, I could do most of the writing at home while my only child was in grade school. Secondly, the weekly deadlines challenged me to look beyond newsworthy events for small epiphanies in my daily efforts.

Weeding my perennial garden, I would suddenly unearth an early memory of my grandparents' backyard in Detroit. Baking bread in my kitchen while U.S. military forces bombed Baghdad, I renewed my commitment to being a peacemaker in my own community. And while recovering from two major surgeries, I realized how many of life's fundamental gifts and simple pleasures I had taken for granted.

In the solitude of my small office at home, I was also forced to take a philosophical look at my pending middle age, the writing life, my father's death, my son's thorny struggle for independence, and what it meant to be a wife, mother, and homemaker in a culture that often marginalized traditional feminine roles. A male newspaper reader, in fact, once told me that his wife always read my Sunday columns—but he didn't. Preferring news and political commentary, he said he wasn't interested "in all that homey stuff." Yet I've always believed that the personal *is* the political, and that what happens in our own homes has a ripple effect on the rest of our world.

Still, column writing was never about persuading readers to embrace my viewpoints. As diarist May Sarton once said, "I have written every poem, every novel, for the same purpose—to find out what I think, to know where I stand." In retrospect, column writing was a tool to help me find the sacred in the suburban, and a way to share my findings with others who were also struggling to fit all the pieces together.

While I didn't realize it at the time, I'd also begun a public diary. Problem was, it didn't look much like a diary. For all the time and ink I'd spent, I only had a stack of yellowing newsprint to show, and my office was starting to look like a recycling bin. I needed a place to store it all—which is a roundabout way of explaining this book.

Originally published between 1992 and 2004, the pieces in this collection are my favorites—the ones I hope my family and friends will want to read again. Many of them first appeared in my hometown newspaper, *The Daily Tribune* of Royal Oak, Michigan, and I am very grateful to all the readers who were engaged in a weekly dialogue with me for more than a decade. Their words of encouragement were a balm on lonely days, and kept me spinning out columns a lot longer than I'd intended.

The essays in this collection are arranged thematically, not chronologically, and a lot has changed since some of the pieces were first published.

For starters, mothers who work at home while raising children are earning a lot more respect for choosing that option now. The vintage Tudor that my husband Doug and I began renovating thirteen years ago finally feels like our own. Our son Nate and his friends, who are often mentioned in my writings, are now away at college. From a national perspective, all of us lost our innocence in the rubble of September 11, 2001, and I doubt that we'll ever recover our sense of small-town security, no matter where we live.

Yet some things haven't changed. Church bells and train whistles still punctuate our daily round. Parents rise early to carpool and get to work on time. Meanwhile, my abiding love for home, family, and community is still the glue that holds my scrapbook together. And I like to believe that our little lives have meaning.

Cindy La Ferle
Royal Oak, Michigan
Thanksgiving 2004

House and Garden

A Woman's Place?

May 8, 1997

C oming of age in the 1970s, I cringed whenever I heard the exhausted adage, "A woman's place is in the home." While the concepts of marriage and motherhood still appealed to me, cleaning up after myself and other people did not.

Throughout my teens, my family expected me to finish college and pursue a career. I was encouraged to be independent and to support myself in a place of my own. But nobody said a word about dusting it.

When we moved into our first apartment in 1980, my architect husband and I never thought to discuss the delicate issue of housework. Devoted to our business careers, Doug and I left early for work every weekday morning, tripping over mounds of unfolded laundry as we headed for the door. We grumbled through domestic chores on Saturdays, never quite sure who was responsible for emptying the trash or disinfecting the toilet bowl.

All of this came tumbling back last summer, when I discovered some old books on housekeeping at a second-hand bookstore. Blowing several layers of dust from their covers, I was rewarded with some fascinating glimpses of early Americana.

First published in 1924, *Good Housekeeping's The Business of Housekeeping*, by Mildred Maddocks Bentley, was a veritable textbook on the domestic arts. Its mildewed, yellowing pages reminded me that household management was once taken very seriously. Speaking to young brides, the book covered such topics as "Managing Servants and Housekeepers," "Dishwashing Three Times a Day," "Sprinkling and Folding," and "The Chemistry of Washing."

As the book's title suggested, Mrs. Bentley meant business: "The good housekeeper must bring to her task of housekeeping every one of the qualities that make for a successful executive in the downtown business world."

A more recent artifact, *Housekeeping Made Simple* (The Homemaker's Encyclopedia, Inc.), was published in 1952. Editor Miriam B. Reichl revealed that, after WWII, women had lightened up a bit and were looking for labor-saving methods. The average housewife, after all, no longer employed domestic help.

Reichl's book contained some amusing black and white photo-illustrations. One showed a woman smiling broadly (and, yes, wearing high heels and pearls) as she demonstrated several ways to use a vacuum. Another shot featured an attractive woman doing laundry in a satin evening gown. Male models were conspicuously absent.

Not one of the women in the photos appeared sweaty or breathless—which is how most of us look today when we are going after dog hair behind the sofa. In fact, the photos seemed to imply that household tasks were glamorous, even fun. The laundry chapter, for instance, was titled "Merrily We Wash."

Years ago, when I was single and rented my first apartment, books devoted to home economics (or "Home Eck" as my girlfriends called it) were rare, although my friends and I could have used a few tips on stocking a pantry or planning balanced meals. Destined for careers, we would leave housework to the cleaning fairies.

Even today, few men or women will admit they *enjoy* doing anything remotely domestic, unless it makes them as rich and famous as Martha Stewart. Like life itself, homemaking is messy business—something you hire other people to do if you can afford it.

"You keep a house, but you make a home," observes anthropology professor Mary Catherine Bateson in *Composing A Life* (Plume/Penguin). "As we free the ideas of home and homemaking from their links to old gender roles, we can now also draw on metaphors of home to enrich our perceptions of the world." Home, after all, is where everyone begins.

While I'd never welcome another era in which women have few career options beyond vacuuming, and I'd hate to see ironing raised to an art form, I think we lose our sense of place—the very foundation that keeps us grounded—when we neglect or denigrate the home front. The driveway becomes a mere parking lot; the kitchen a place to park an empty fridge. The house exudes an atmosphere as impersonal as a chain motel.

But lately I've noticed a new crop of "homecare" guides in local bookstores. These books are saturated with a deep yearning for roots and shelter. And unlike their predecessors, the books seem to be devoid of sexism, though women will most likely buy them. Whether or not Americans will embrace a homemaking revival remains to be seen.

Right now, we're still arguing over whose turn it is to clean the bathroom.

———————

Home Sweet Office

September 10, 1994

"I have to guard against allowing myself to be defined, either by myself or by others, in traditional, sociological terms."
—Anne Truitt, *Daybook: The Journey of an Artist*

I suppose you could say I'm moving up in the world, since my writing studio is no longer annexed to the laundry room in our basement. Last year I acquired a handsome cherry-wood desk and a first-floor room with a view.

On my desk I've arranged a few of my treasures, including a framed photo of my son when he was four. On a shelf nearby, in the shadow of my computer, an Underwood manual typewriter adds a touch of decorative irony. And in plain view, I've posted a favorite quote: "In every moment, we find ourselves at the crossroads of Here and Now."

The here and now—my son's childhood, in particular—is why I decided several years ago to practice journalism from home. And while I can't imagine writing anywhere else now, it took a few years and several crossroads to arrive at this place.

Like Dorothy, I used to think Oz was anywhere but home. After college, I was employed in the production department of a large reference book publisher, where I learned that producing books for other writers wasn't nearly as much fun as trying to write your own. Later, during a five-year stint as a travel magazine editor, I was given rented office space at a large chemical company. Visitors were always alarmed to discover that the tiny rooms in which my staff and I worked often smelled of acetone or sulfur, which wafted from the laboratory across the hall. Luckily, that job also required several weeks of travel to bed-and-breakfast inns around the country, so I also learned how to pack a suitcase and build a wrinkle-free career wardrobe.

Meanwhile, with a small child at home, I had dreams of combining parenthood with freelance journalism. And while I wasn't quite ready to surrender travel writing and regular paychecks, fate had other plans. Before my son turned six, the travel magazine folded, thanks to sagging advertising revenues. Journalism jobs in the Detroit area, where I live, were hard to land, thanks to an historic newspaper strike. And so, while it sounded daring to my corporate friends, my big move down to the damp basement of our 1920s home was also my last resort.

Luckily I had a handful of promising editorial contacts and, gratefully, my husband's financial support. Writing, I told myself, was something you could easily do at home while your kid was napping or building Lego castles.

I was wrong about the easy part.

To the parent who's eager to combine office work with housekeeping, setting up shop at a kid's craft table next to the laundry room might sound convenient. But this was not what Virginia Woolf had in mind when she wrote about claiming a room of one's own. Working in my basement was a metaphor for the way I undervalued my work at the time.

I also found it difficult to split myself cheerfully between Professional Writer and Perfect Mom. My desk in the basement was frequently littered with my son's early science experiments. Settling in to write, I'd find blue finger paint or Play-Doh oozing from my paper-clip container. My scissors and rolls of tape mysteriously disappeared. Meanwhile, the dryer kept buzzing.

Following intense negotiations, my son and I reviewed the definition of *boundaries* and why it was essential to establish them. A good lesson for us both.

Now that I've moved my office upstairs to a small den at the end of the house, I take myself, and my work, more seriously. My son, who's still in grade school, respects my new office, and usually remembers to ask before he borrows my supplies.

That said, my income as a freelance newspaper columnist and magazine writer is several thousand dollars short of what it was when I was employed full-time. Thankfully, the family has agreed to lower their financial expectations. But I have to remind myself that my worth as a person isn't calculated by paychecks.

Several working mothers in my neighborhood—the sharp-looking ones who drive off to work in designer suits every morning at 7:00—are a little suspicious of my lifestyle. I know some of them wonder if I'm at the mall every day.

So here's my advice to other stay-at-home mothers: Forget what other people think and guard your time with your life, because a lot more is expected from women who work at home. (Casseroles, clean bathrooms, car pools, free baby-sitting, moral support, and cupcakes for the school bake sale are supposed to be a cinch when you've got all that "extra time" on your hands.) If you can afford it, hire a sitter to help. And for heaven's sake, learn to say no.

There's no getting around the fact that home can get lonely. A freelancer often misses out on promotions as well as office camaraderie, and you rarely get invited to office Christmas parties. I celebrated by myself, for example, on the day I learned that I won first place in a statewide newspaper column contest. But I have no regrets.

"My motherhood has been, I realize, central to my life as a stove is central to a household in the freeze of winter," writes sculptor Anne Truitt in *Daybook: The Journey of an Artist* (Penguin Books). "And I am accustomed to sustaining the effort of my work by offsetting it with the lovely affections of family life."

I love the weekday mornings best. After my husband and son leave for work and school, I pour my first cup of coffee and straighten my desk. Before I begin my first hour of writing, I look out my office windows and watch for neighbors. There's always a parade of devoted walkers—mostly retirees and a few young moms with babies in tow. An older gentleman sometimes looks toward my window and waves, silently acknowledging the kinship we share on these clear, bright mornings.

Time passes quickly when the writing is going well. And before long, the back door bursts open and my son is home from school, sometimes with a friend.

"Hey Mom! Where are you?" Within minutes, our once-quiet household throbs with new energy, and I head for the kitchen to begin my second shift.

Not long ago, another writer called to let me know there were a couple of openings at a newspaper office. "One has your name on it," she pressed. "You interested?"

The pay and benefits sounded tempting, though the hours were long. I knew I had a good shot at one of the openings, but it didn't take long for me to say no; that I'd already landed the job of a lifetime.

———————

Does Lurch Live Here?

August 30, 1992

M ost people have the common sense to buy houses that are younger than they are.

They sleep snugly under leak-free roofs, secure in the knowledge that if something goes bump in the night, it probably isn't the heating system. Their homes are airtight sanctuaries of Pella windows, state-of-the-art plumbing, and bubbling Jacuzzis.

To homeowners with such modern sensibilities, my family's 1920s Tudor-style home looks like a gloomy architectural relic, all dark woodwork and creaky floorboards. A place only the Addams family could love.

"I can't believe people really live in these old places," gasped one visitor who recently toured the house.

Throughout our twelve married years together, my husband and I have always purchased houses built before 1947. We've searched, begged, and borrowed to get them. We've tolerated cracked plaster, peeling paint, damp basements, and antique toilets. We've put up with steam pipes that clank and moan after midnight like Marley's ghost.

Are we crazy? Why would we choose to live in an old house, subjecting ourselves to outrageous repair bills and leaded-glass windows that rattle in the slightest breeze?

I'm never quite sure how to explain my own passion for houses with a past. But I can trace its beginnings to my childhood vacations, when my parents drove me to Colonial Williamsburg and Mount Vernon. While other kids rode roller coasters in Disneyland, I snooped around George Washington's bedroom. Early on, I discovered that buildings, like people, acquire nobility and character as they mature.

Old houses are survivors. They possess a mystique that seems to say, "I've been here long enough to see some things that you haven't." And the best ones persevere despite the "improvements" inflicted upon them over the decades by various owners with questionable taste. Brick and stone prevail; solid architecture endures.

I'm also drawn to the history that comes with an older house; I'm intrigued by the everyday romance of the people and events that have become a part of its mortar and plaster. In fact, buying an older house usually has nothing to do with common sense—and everything to do with history and romance. In a way, choosing a house that someone else has lived in is a bit like choosing a marriage partner: You grow to love the bumps and flaws, and accept the things you cannot change. (People who insist on having everything their own way should design new houses.)

My husband and I bought our first old house from an elderly woman named Gertrude Morris, an endearing elderly woman who was reluctant at first to put her place on the market. She had years of memories tucked away in her kitchen cupboards and bedroom closets, and her late husband had left a legacy of wildflowers and wayward groundcover in the backyard.

After the closing, our real estate agent confided that Mrs. Morris "liked" us. So she graciously surrendered the keys to the door that had sheltered her family for so many years. She had agreed to a land contract with us, so she was, in a way, still keeper of those keys.

I remember sending her a monthly house report with each payment. One time I told her about the red calico wallpaper I struggled to put up in our cramped kitchen; another time I wrote about the bright pink sweet peas I uncovered during my first spring in the garden.

Mrs. Morris couldn't always respond. But one Christmas she answered, in a wavering hand, that she was pleased we were taking such good care of the house. After she died, I heard that she had looked forward to my letters in the nursing home. They were an important link to a place that mattered to both of us.

It's been several years since we sold "Mrs. Morris's house," but I drive by it sometimes, just to be sure its new owners are taking care of it.

We've lived in our 1920s Tudor for just over a year now—long enough to see the silver maples on the lawn change through a full cycle of seasons. But not long enough for the neighbors to think of this as our place. That will happen as our lives weave slowly into the fabric of the neighborhood, when our past becomes a longer chapter in the history of the house.

My son, now six, is learning to appreciate older houses, too. He can call some of them by their proper names: Cape Cod, Tudor, Dutch Colonial. He is just beginning to understand the inevitable progression of time, and how buildings connect us to the people who lived before us.

And my boy has become quite the preservationist, putting old things to clever new uses. When he and his friends come inside after playing in the snow, he shows them how to dry their soggy gloves on a cast-iron radiator in the hallway. During one of these winter rituals, I overheard him lecturing another child on the virtues of radiators and steam heat.

"Steam heat is the greatest heat there is, and you won't find these big old radiators in new houses," he boasted. "That's because old houses are better than new ones."

A mother with more common sense would have tactfully interrupted the conversation, and assured both children that old houses are not necessarily better than new ones.

I didn't say a word.

Zen and Remodeling

January 18, 2003

"We are always in transition.
If you can just relax with that, you'll have no problem."
—Pema Chodron, Buddhist nun

The construction crew hasn't even started yet, but I'm already bracing myself for several weeks of chaos and plaster dust.

Half of our clothes and most of our toiletries have been temporarily stashed in other regions of the house. With the exception of our master bedroom, in fact, everything upstairs is in a state of minor upheaval. I hate living like this.

It's all in preparation for our next remodeling project, which includes new plumbing, tile, and fixtures for our circa 1926 bathroom, plus expanded closet space and a paint job for the spare bedroom. The crew is scheduled to begin this week, but that's just what they tell me. Until I see trucks in the driveway, I know better than to count on anything. Being married to an architect and having survived several remodeling projects, I now have a grasp of what I call "building trade ethics."

Even in the most professional situations, building trade ethics bear little resemblance to the Protestant work ethic. For starters, people in the building trades do not follow a nine-to-five schedule. These guys have their own system, and it's up to you to figure out what that is.

They also speak a different language. For example, if the plumber who's installing your new toilet says he'll be back to finish at noon on Friday, it's possible that he really means *maybe sometime on a Friday next month.*

With few exceptions, though, the results are worth it. If you love your old house as much as we love ours, you realize that a disrupted schedule is a small price to pay for the lifestyle improvements you'll get eventually.

And if you really want to feel smug, you can tell yourself that your renovation project is also for posterity. Fixing up an old house is a gift to the community—which is why I cringe every time someone tears down a perfectly decent old home, only to replace it with a brand-new Big Foot palace. But that's a topic for another time.

Right now, I'm trying to focus on the positive. Compared to one of our last projects—a kitchen makeover and a sun room that took nine months to complete—this next effort should be a piece of cake.

Still, every time our walls give way to a sledge hammer, I'm reminded that change is messy. More often than not, you must tear something apart and disrupt your routine to make things better. You can't install a new shower, for instance, without uprooting the old one. You can't hang new wallpaper over old wallpaper and expect to end up with a smooth, bubble-free finish. And you must never varnish a hardwood floor before sanding away its stained or splintered imperfections.

Likewise, you can't sugarcoat the rigors of self-improvement.

Come January, everyone wants to be thinner, healthier, wiser, smoke-free, and less wrinkly. And we'd like to achieve these goals as quickly as possible, preferably with a single-dose pill that works while we're asleep.

But self-improvement takes time and willpower, which is why some of us give up before we've hit the target. As every dieter knows, the "in between sizes" stage—the first plateau—is the trickiest. The process is ongoing, arduous, and more than an act of faith.

My dear old house is also a work in progress. It has taught me how to be patient and how to make sense of the chaos that precedes any kind of transformation. With a little luck, I think we can survive another month of plaster dust together.

So, bring on the building crew. Whenever.

———————

Summer Home

I t began in June with a large cardboard box, just roomy enough to house my wiry eight-year-old son, Nate, and a scrap of old tweed carpeting.

"The fort," as Nate dubbed it, was expanded throughout the summer to include several new rooms, each designed from salvaged appliance boxes of various shapes and sizes. By the time it was finished, the fort curled like a corrugated snake across the entire lawn. Other kids in our neighborhood added their own flourishes—round windows, paper awnings and banners, plastic pipes and tubes. (Whether these served functional or aesthetic purposes, only the children knew.)

By the end of July, Nate's cardboard Xanadu had become something of a local landmark. It was such hot property, in fact, that you had to write your name on the official SIGN-UP SHEET to be admitted inside, a bit like the exclusive restaurants lining Main Street downtown.

Since we live on a corner lot in a carefully maintained suburb, I worried that our neighbors would object to the ever-growing mountain of boxes in our yard. If you had no imagination and didn't know you were looking at a playhouse, you might have guessed we were careless about storing our trash.

But no one complained. Other parents who had watched the fort's progress were amazed to see that something as simple and economical as a stack of empty appliance boxes could keep so many children amused for so long. One afternoon, a local building contractor even stopped his truck to admire the fort's design.

"Hey there, that's quite a place!" he called out to Nate and his pals. "Are you renting space in your cardboard condo?" But the kids insisted they weren't looking for more tenants.

"Every spirit builds itself a house, and beyond its house a world, and beyond its world a heaven," wrote Ralph Waldo Emerson. We're born with the desire to create a home, to build our own retreat. And while home can mean something different to everyone, the need for a sense of place is universally human. To a small boy, a discarded carton contains unlimited potential for a playhouse or a fortress of his own.

But to the homeless man who camps near the railroad tracks at the edge of our town, a cardboard box might be his only refuge.

Nate and I first spotted the shelter a few weeks after his fort was built. We were heading toward our favorite fast-food restaurant downtown, taking our time as we walked along a gravel service road flanking the railroad tracks.

The two of us noticed a crude assemblage of large boxes almost hidden behind a tangle of wild thistle and Queen Anne's lace. Torn blankets and soiled clothing were strung on branches nearby; long sheets of blue plastic encircled the base of the boxes like small rivers. Right away, Nate noticed that the makeshift shelter looked remarkably like his cardboard fort back home.

"What's all the plastic for, and why does the man live there instead of a real house?" he asked as we walked past the encampment. I explained that the homeless man probably used the plastic to keep the boxes dry when it rained. But I didn't know how to explain the complexities of being homeless to a suburban second-grader who is tucked securely into bed on a full stomach every night.

Following a heat wave later that week, a powerful evening storm rolled in. It brewed so quickly that my husband and I didn't have time to pull Nate's fort into the garage. By morning it was scattered across the lawn. Even "the turret," a sturdy refrigerator carton in its previous life, had toppled like an uprooted tree among the soggy ruins.

At first I was secretly relieved that we could finally dismantle all the boxes that had taken over our yard. But Nate was fighting tears as he tried to salvage parts of his handiwork, and I couldn't help but feel his loss. Together we folded the sheets of rain-soaked cardboard and piled them near the trash in our garage.

Since then, school has started again. But we haven't discarded a cardboard box without seriously considering its possibilities. And we often wonder about the homeless man who had set up camp near the railroad tracks. The last time we walked there, we noticed that his shelter, like Nate's fort, had collapsed in the hard summer rain.

———————

Trowel and Error

A fter all these years, I still can't muster the nerve to call myself a real gardener.

Real gardeners understand that a garden is an ecosystem as well as an art form.

Real gardeners spend hours studying seed catalogs, and can identify every plant in the nursery by its botanical name. Always victorious in the battle against slugs, real gardeners are attuned to nature's early warning signs and know exactly what to do when leaves turn yellow.

A real gardener I am not—but I'm getting there.

Gardening as a metaphor for living is a cliché as old as the gardens at Versailles. But I just turned fifty this year, and it occurs to me that plotting my life's course has been as tricky as maintaining the perennial beds I started a few years ago. My garden has provided clues along the way.

A Midwest native, I've always lived in established neighborhoods with mature trees, so I've had to seek out plants that will tolerate plenty of shade and depleted soil. Even now, I'm still experimenting, still trying to get it right.

Bob and Jane, my elder neighbors across the street, have watched my green experiments from their porch and offered advice. They often catch me watering a newly transplanted hosta or puttering around the herb beds in my pajamas on sunny mornings. Returning from vacation one summer, they brought me a ceramic garden marker that reads, "Gardens grow by trowel and error," which pretty much sums it up.

In my early years of home ownership, I followed a much safer path.

Back then, I planted only what a master gardener would call "amateur annuals." In my own defense, I was trying to raise a child while working at home. I wrote shorter newspaper articles—never had the nerve to start a novel—and barely had time to fuss with a potted geranium, let alone a crop of needy, exotic perennials.

I was also a house-proud perfectionist, always worried that I'd be judged by my foliage and found inferior. Afraid of taking risks, I aimed for an instant gratification garden—a showy but conventional patch that didn't require much care. But now that I'm more adventurous and, well, less pot-bound, I'm finally reaping the rewards of an unruly perennial garden.

For starters, a struggling peony I planted three years ago produced several crimson flowers for the first time this spring. The blooms are gone, but I'm still gloating.

By nature I'm not a patient person. I hate waiting in line and sometimes I'm too fidgety to meditate. But my stalled peony bush taught me a crucial life lesson: There are times when the best plan of action is to wait and see what happens. Seeds germinate and flower on their own schedule, and natural processes can't be rushed. (Like that novel I want to start.)

Last year, in fact, I had almost given up on the poor peony and was ready to move it, which would have been a big mistake. Like me, it was just a late bloomer that needed a little more time, and faith, to take root.

For a day or so, I was tempted to cut those gorgeous peony blooms and bring them indoors to enjoy in a crystal vase. But since I'm still a show-off, I left them outside for all the neighbors to admire.

———————————

Trees and Memories

May 24, 2004

Trees add so much more than shade and property value to our homes.

Last week, on the boulevard across the street, a trio of Bradford pear trees burst into snowy bloom. Surrounded by smaller stands of lilac, the pear trees are the first to flower. I look forward to their annual display in late April, and am always relieved when I return from spring vacation to see I haven't missed it.

While it might not seem like such a big deal to anyone else, I'm proud of this contribution to my neighborhood landscape.

My little grove began with a single tree, which I ordered from the City of Royal Oak the first spring in our present home. In subsequent years I added two more Bradford pears. Today, everyone in our immediate family is represented by a flowering tree.

Like the three of us, each tree has filled out over the past twelve years—a natural reminder of how quickly we're all changing. Nate was in kindergarten when the first spindly tree was planted, and in two weeks he'll graduate high school. Come fall, the foliage on our pear trees will turn bright orange, then crimson. And just as I do every year, I'll admire the color show from our dining room window and console myself with the fact that everything, including the landscape, is evolving right on schedule.

But in our backyard now, there's a newly vacant space where a magnificent white pine once stood.

The pine had set down roots several years before we moved here. During a visit with our home's previous owners, we learned that the pine—which had split into three distinct trunks—was a monument to the family's three children. They told us they'd named it The Trinity Tree, and had even buried a beloved pet beneath it.

Sadly, their Trinity Tree started dropping needles and showing other signs of stress two summers ago, but neither my husband nor I knew how to save it.

And I wasn't ready to take it down. Around its base I had planted what I called a "sacred garden" of lilies and bleeding heart, complete with a small statue of St. Anthony. I especially enjoyed this view of The Trinity Tree from the sunroom. By this time, it had established itself as part of my own family's history, too.

But last month a tree specialist confirmed the pine was dead and had to go. Fighting tears, I watched from the sunroom window as a team of workers methodically severed all three trunks, section by section, and removed them from the yard. Later, while pulling Saint Anthony from the rubble, I remembered he is the patron saint of barrenness and lost articles.

Citing a recent study conducted by the University of Illinois, Maria Rodale noted in *Organic Style* magazine that people who live near trees have stronger family ties than those who live in treeless areas. "Trees create a sanctuary around us," Rodale noted. "They certainly make us feel grounded and safe."

I'm not sure what I'll plant to replace The Trinity Tree and the trampled garden left behind. This is a fragile time. For now, I'm preparing for Nate's graduation and savoring the last of the blossoms on the pear trees before they give way to summer's sturdier foliage.

The Long Way Home

September 20, 2001

A little more than a week has passed since our country was attacked and brought to its knees.

A friend of mine says she is trying to wake up from what she calls Stephen King's worst nightmare. The rest of us still feel as though we've been wandering in a fog, unable to find our way home. Home, it seems, has been completely redesigned by horrific acts of terrorism. Ever since last Tuesday, everything is different. Everything.

I have stopped assuming that home will ever be completely safe from disaster. This thought alone makes every wall, every window, every piece of oak, maple, brick, or concrete in my neighborhood, my world, seem all the more precious.

I've also stopped obsessing over the things I used to obsess about. I've stopped worrying about the fact that my refrigerator needs cleaning and the walls in the kitchen need repainting. Things like that don't matter now. My focus has changed.

It doesn't matter if my family leaves a mess on the breakfast counter every morning. And so what if I trip over somebody's shoes in the hallway? I am deeply grateful that there are people living here—eating breakfast and wearing shoes.

I imagine this is all part of the grieving process, and that some-day things will seem normal again. Right now, though, I feel a bit like Emily in Thornton Wilder's *Our Town*. Emily is the character who, near the end of the play, returns to her hometown as a ghost and realizes how much she took for granted when she was alive. Emily recites a list of the simple things that made her days precious—things like the smell of freshly brewed coffee in the morning.

I know exactly what she meant. This week I'm savoring the taste of summer's last tomatoes. I'm taking time to watch the sun set behind the maples in our yard, and to listen to the sound of cathedral bells just a few blocks away.

But I can't think of anyone who is appreciating the comforts of home as much as Norma Gormly of Troy, Michigan.

Norma's plane was diverted back to London's Gatwick Airport immediately following the terrorist attacks on the World Trade Center and the Pentagon.

Norma and her daughter, Jan, had been on vacation and ended up stranded at a bed-and-breakfast inn outside London until the air-ways were cleared for their return to the United States. Theirs was the first Northwest flight to leave last Friday. As Norma told me, it was quite an experience.

"We had to go through four checkpoints and check in all bags," she recalled. "We were allowed our purses with personal stuff only. Following a body search, we were admitted to the lounge area."

None of the passengers complained, though, even though their wait was long. Another three hours passed before their flight left Gatwick.

"We felt good that they had done all that they could for our safety,"

Norma said. "We had the same flight crew from our diverted plane."

That crew, Norma recalled, wore black ribbons around the gold wings on their uniforms. Some were fighting tears, "but they all promised to do their best to make our trip as normal as possible. Our captain was informative and soothing."

Norma and her fellow passengers clapped and cheered loudly as their plane finally took off. They cheered again when the plane passed over Canada. And it was, as Norma remembers, a tremendous relief to arrive back home in America.

"We cheered and clapped, then cheered and clapped again upon landing at Metro Airport. We were home at last!"

No matter what shape it's in, Norma added, there's no place like home. Home is a word every American cherishes—more than ever, now.

———————

Child Care

Quit Picking on Barbie

December 12, 1997

As a journalist who frequently writes about women's issues, I've lost patience with people who accuse Mattel's Barbie doll of being a bad influence on growing girls. Worst of all, Mattel is melting under pressure, promising to deliver a new Barbie doll with more realistic proportions next year.

It all amounts to a tempest in a Barbie-size teacup. And besides, why pick on Barbie when we have bigger, real-life offenders to fry?

Growing up with Barbie, I never thought her original statistics (38-18-34, according to one estimate) were a threat to my self-esteem. In fact, I've gotten a kick out of Barbie ever since I first played with her in the 1960s, just when the feminist movement was gaining momentum. And I think Gloria Steinem would have approved of the way my Barbie and Midge dolls carved out their futures.

In the fantasy world I crafted for them, both dolls attended good colleges. (They packed wardrobes they'd earned by working part-time in their cardboard clothing boutique.) Even then, their career options weren't limited to traditional female careers. Barbie and Midge studied math and medicine as well as fashion design. Barbie had plans to be an astronaut, Midge a veterinarian. I imagine, too, that both were even prepared to "sequence" their careers if ever they decided to marry and have children.

My Barbie and Midge were also well versed in the fine arts. They performed in several Broadway plays and musicals, including *Camelot*, staged on the Little Theater I had been given for my tenth birthday. Midge earned standing ovations as Little Red Riding Hood, while Ken took on the dubious role of Big Bad Wolf.

I have other happy memories of playing with Mattel's fold-up Dream House, which Barbie had mortgaged herself and kept clean while holding down several part-time jobs (in addition to her college classes). After she earned her driver's license, I helped her navigate her own pink convertible along the highways she forged in my parents' living room carpet.

Yes, the road was wide open for Barbie. She was the first to have it all—and the first to dress for success. More than any other doll on the toy store shelves, Barbie had choices beyond hearth and home. If nothing else, she showed us that a woman could do anything she wanted to, and that looking fabulous was just another bonus. Examining the doll today, I don't see that this has changed.

For today's parents, the big dilemma seems to be the doll's figure—long legs, skinny waist, narrow hips, ample bosom. They worry that her stiff plastic body flaunts impossible standards for young girls to emulate. But are little girls really that gullible? Most kids I know understand that toys aren't supposed to be fully realistic. Pretending is the whole point. After all, the thirty-eight-year-old Barbie always has been touted as a fashion doll, and half the fun of a fashion doll is the sheer fantasy of dressing her in all kinds of uniforms and costumes, from tiny space suits to jazzy evening gowns.

As long as Barbie's new body is just as much fun to dress, I suppose there's no harm in rearranging her parts. But I knew many girls who enjoyed Barbie in her original form, and ultimately soared to adulthood undamaged by their favorite doll's controversial figure.

Even now, many of us secretly admire Barbie for being exactly what she is—a gal with options who never takes herself too seriously.

———————

Cider Stand

I t was one of those luminous Indian summer afternoons—clear cobalt skies and pure yellow light shimmering through the maples on our front lawn. This was autumn's last hurrah, and even the neighborhood kids sensed the day was ripe for celebrating.

I'd taken the day off work and suggested we drive to the old cider mill in Franklin Village, where it's always worth standing in line for the best cinnamon doughnuts made in Michigan. But Nate, who was six at the time, had his own ideas. He and Catie, the girl next door, would set up their own cider-and-doughnuts stand in our front yard, which faces a well-traveled boulevard.

Naturally, I ended up at the local fruit market, loading a shopping cart with doughnuts and several gallons of apple cider.

Back home, I retrieved a card table and some cardboard for a poster, then rallied the kids to assemble the doughnuts and paper cups on a serving tray. The three of us positioned the cider stand at the corner of our front yard.

The small entrepreneurs perched on lawn chairs and waited patiently for customers. They waved at passing cars and periodically rearranged the paper cups. Business was painfully slow.

Watching the eager pair from the front porch, I felt my heart skip each time a car sped past them. Surely some generous adult would step on the brakes, reach deep into a pocket, and pull out a dime for a cool cup of cider. But most drivers didn't seem to notice.

I've been guilty of similar oversights. Rushing to the office, the bank, or an appointment, I've driven past countless children trying to earn spare change at their sidewalk stands. Sometimes I rolled down the window and promised to catch them on my way back, at my convenience, which was usually too late.

Slowly but surely, my faith in humanity was restored as a few neighbors came around to patronize the cider stand. Quarters, dimes, and nickels clinked musically in the collection cup, while Nate and Catie whirled around the card table.

And I'll never forget how stunned the pair looked when a stranger pulled up in a red convertible with the top down, radio blaring. Leaping from the car, the man sprinted up to the table, grabbed one of the cups, and downed his cider in one memorable gulp. He smiled as he stuffed a bill into the collection cup, and didn't wait for his change. As the stranger roared down the boulevard, the children flew to me on the front porch, chirping like startled sparrows all the way up the steps.

"Guess what! That guy in the car gave us ten dollars for the cider and he didn't want any change!! *TEN DOLLARS!!*"

Breathless and giddy, the two began negotiating how the miraculous windfall would be divided. One of them remarked that the cider must have been very good, having earned such an awesome profit.

Despite everything that's wrong in the world, it's hard to remain cynical on a grace-filled day like that. I remembered a phrase I'd read by the poet John Keats, and I knew that this was what he meant by "Moments big as years."

Don't Worry, Mom!

August 6, 1995

Nate is away for the weekend, visiting a water park in Muskegon.

He's traveling with Alex, a best buddy from school, and his family. Alex's mom gave me the address and phone number of the Holiday Inn where they will be staying. And I have a list detailing their itinerary.

"Don't worry, Mom," were Nate's parting words. He could hardly wait to go.

A man of the world at nine years old, Nate left hauling a backpack stuffed with his terrycloth bathrobe, a bathing suit, two changes of clothing, a new travel-size toothbrush and tube of toothpaste, a paperback copy of *The Unbelievable Adventures of Pecos Bill*, and the full roll of quarters I'd given him for emergency phone calls.

Before the trip I lectured him on the dangers of wandering off by himself. "*Always* stay with Alex's family," I repeated several times.

"You worry too much, Mom," he said, rolling his eyes.

I know, I know. I shouldn't worry at all. And I remind myself that this isn't the first time he's traveled without his dad and me; my in-laws have even taken him Up North to their cottage several times. Nate relishes the personal freedom in these adventures, and I know they're great experiences for him.

And I hope he has fun in Muskegon. I remember being allowed to take overnight trips with my friends when I was his age. In particular, I loved visiting the farmhouse owned by my best friend's grandmother in Caro, where we explored open fields all day and stayed up half the night chasing fireflies.

But like most moms I know, I still worry. I still envision worst-case scenarios. In the murky corners of my imagination lurk the unspeakable monsters every parent fears, from drunk drivers on the expressway to kidnappers at the concession stands.

"Don't worry, Mom."

I try to squelch these nightmares as quickly as they surface, reassuring myself that most people are trustworthy and the world isn't really as awful as it looks on the evening news. Like every conscientious parent I know, I'm just learning how to let go; how to loosen my grip on the poor child's backpack.

The lessons begin very early, starting with the first time we leave a child with a baby-sitter or at preschool. Soon after, there's the first day of kindergarten, then the first day of grade school. Our throats tighten as the school door snaps shut and another chapter of childhood begins.

For stay-at-home moms, the youngest child's first day of school is fraught with conflicting bouts of loneliness and exhilarating autonomy. We're finally free to redesign our schedules according to our own needs. We can turn off "Mister Rogers" and "Sesame Street." But there are times when the stillness brushes our shoulders like a sudden autumn chill. Without children, the house sounds too hollow.

This, to me, is the irony in raising kids: When they're small and constantly tugging on our sleeves, we crave some breathing space for ourselves. When they're older and backing out of the driveway, we hope they'll hurry back.

So far, Nate's dad and I have enjoyed our time alone this weekend. We've finished some neglected chores. We've held long conversations without being interrupted by a breathless nine-year-old whose burning interest of the moment is stamp collecting. We've eaten in restaurants that do not offer complimentary crayons or serve grilled cheese sandwiches. For now, there are no Lego blocks and empty juice boxes scattered across the living room floor.

And finally, I have stopped worrying about the boy whose temporary absence accounts for these radical changes in our lifestyle. But I haven't stopped missing him.

Mother and Son Answer the Call of the Wild

August 11, 1996

T hanks to my previous career as a travel editor, I know how to rate a mattress and a motel bathroom. I'm right at home in a wicker rocker on the porch of a quiet country inn, sipping a tall glass of iced tea while watching the sun dip behind a mountain range.

But until my son joined Cub Scouts two years ago, my getaways did not include wilderness adventures. To me, communing with nature meant reading Thoreau or maybe potting begonias. So spending a weekend in the woods of rural Michigan—with a chorus of bull frogs, sundry snakes, ticks, two dozen little boys and their suburban-Detroit mothers—didn't sound like my idea of a good time.

Like most parents, however, I've learned to adapt.

And while I am not exactly what you'd call a happy camper, the Scouts have taught me to appreciate the Great Outdoors. In fact, this fall I'll embark on my third annual "Mom & Me" camping weekend with Nate's pack. (These weekends were devised to encourage mother-and-son bonding, and to refute the theory that women will not sleep with insects.)

I've also learned that the travel writer's motto, "Always pack light," doesn't apply to north woods camping. On our first outing, for instance, Nate fell into a bog within fifteen minutes of our arrival at the camp site. He had to borrow my hiking boots until his own dried out the next day. Meanwhile, I had no choice but to tour the swamp in soggy tennis shoes.

"This weekend is an endurance test for parents," one mom confided, half-seriously.

The following year I stuffed half a dozen pairs of boots into the back of our Jeep, but forgot my own raincoat. Of course, that was the weekend it poured and poured…and poured.

I'll never forget the sight of six devoted moms building a campfire in the evening drizzle. (We were determined to do this thing right: We were going to roast every single hot dog and melt every marshmallow we'd hauled along with our Dura-flame logs.) Our boys, however, were smart enough to hide from the rain. Searching the campground by flashlight, we finally found them in one of the cabins playing Life, the board game of the moment.

"Bring the hot dogs in here," one nine-year-old demanded as he scooted his car-shaped marker across the board. "I'm getting ready to sell one of my houses and I'm having a midlife crisis!"

If we're very lucky, the hike to the public restrooms is only fifteen minutes (uphill) from our campsite. The trick, I found, is to keep a spare flashlight in your sleeping bag so that you can grab it quickly if nature calls at 2:00 A.M.

Nobody sleeps much on these weekends. The kids are buzzing on caffeine, having consumed several gallons of Pepsi and Mountain Dew. The moms, smelling like a bonfire and desperately wishing for one hot shower, toss fitfully in their sleeping bags while the boys play flashlight games and tell ghost stories.

"Did you hear the one about the one-eyed man who went berserk in the north woods and was NEVER FOUND...?"

After two nights like these, the long drive back on Sunday is tolerable only with a mug of instant coffee and the promise of a warm bath. Completely exhausted, Nate and I usually ride home in silence.

But last October, on the way home he mumbled, "Thanks for the weekend, Mom...Great weekend." It was a rare moment of sincere, unprompted gratitude.

Catching a glimpse of myself in the rearview mirror, I remembered I wasn't wearing makeup. My eyes looked older, and in an instant I saw the years racing past me like the cars on the expressway. My boy looked older, too, his lanky body slouched on the seat next to me.

Suddenly, that weekend—my endurance test—seemed awfully short. I was proud of myself for hiking swamps and building fires in the rain.

———————

Why Parents Should Be Invisible

June 26, 2001

There comes a time in every mother's life when she realizes parts of her wardrobe shouldn't be flaunted in front of teenage boys. And I'm not talking about thong underwear.

This hit me a couple of years ago while the family and I were getting ready to visit my favorite local art fair—an annual summer event that typically draws crowds of creative types, including some neighbors we haven't seen all winter. Naturally, I wanted to dress for the occasion. Scouring my closet, I chose a nice black T-shirt and an ankle-length peasant skirt. It was a departure from my traditional blazer-with-jeans uniform, but still within the bounds of good taste.

Or so I thought.

The silver bracelet is what got me in trouble. Rescued from a flea-market, the vintage cuff was two inches wide and etched with a subtle ethnic design. Not all that remarkable—unless, of course, you were looking at it through the discerning eyes of an adolescent boy.

"You're not wearing that giant bracelet in public, are you?" asked Nate, glaring at my wrist.

"Why not?" I shot back.

"You look like a Babylonian. Or, maybe a barbarian," Nate said, choosing his words carefully. A week earlier he told me that my feet looked "Cro-Magnon" in sandals. Apparently I'd morphed into a badly dressed savage.

What could I do?

When the same kid was a cranky infant, I couldn't treat his diaper rash without consulting a stack of childcare guides. Soon enough, though, Doug and I were navigating the choppy waters of parenthood without much advice from Penelope Leach or T. Berry Brazelton. Living by our wits, we maneuvered somehow through mealtime face-offs and nerve-racking episodes with the neighborhood bully. We even managed to steer a fairly civilized carpool. But things changed when our little boy began slouching toward adolescence. We needed more help from the experts.

Just in time, Doug found a copy of Anthony Wolf's aptly titled guide, *Get Out of My Life, but First Could You Drive Me and Cheryl to the Mall?* (Noonday Press). As the author notes, today's youth "are vastly different" from kids forty years ago. Just for starters, their social and academic pressures are more complicated, more intense.

"Teen-agers treat adults in their lives in a manner that is less automatically obedient, much more fearless, and definitely more outspoken than that of previous generations," writes Wolf, who happens to be a parent as well as a clinical psychologist.

Many adolescents, he says, feel trapped between the growing need for independence and the secret wish to cling to childhood—an agonizing conflict if ever there was one.

"The two main forces of adolescence are the onset of sexuality and the mandate that demands that teen-agers turn away from childhood and parents," Wolf writes. Not only do teen-agers see their parents as grossly flawed, he adds, "they also find them outright embarrassing, especially if seen with them anywhere outside the home."

This explains why your teen-ager will hug you in the kitchen when nobody is looking but never, ever, in the school parking lot. Or why he ridicules your impeccable fashion sense.

Other moms assure me that this too shall pass. Even the mouthiest teens can grow up to be agreeable, well-adjusted human beings. In the meantime they need our patience, our love, and a healthy dose of discipline.

But patience can be the hardest part, especially for barbarians.

———————————

A Mother's Prayer

December 10, 2000

"It's a long road from conception to completion."
—Moliere

L ord, help me. Nate is taking in a three-week driver's education course this month after school. The very thought of it makes me carsick.

Last week I browsed through the materials he is studying for the class. Compiled by the State of Michigan, one handbook is titled *What Every Driver Must Know*, and the introduction contains a list of sobering statistics.

The numbers reported are slightly outdated now, but readers are duly reminded that more than 142,000 people in Michigan are seriously injured, and approximately 1,500 people are killed, annually, in traffic crashes. In 1996, we're told, one person was injured every three minutes and forty-one seconds in a car accident. And as if that weren't grisly enough, we're warned that "traffic crashes are the leading cause of accidental death for people ages one to twenty-four years." I am not sure how (or if) this information impacts young drivers in training, but it's enough to send any mother into a tailspin.

So maybe I'm a tad overprotective.

I remind myself that it will be months before Nate is eligible to drive without adult supervision; his driver's training class is only

46

the first step toward earning his permit. And it's not that I don't trust him. My son is a responsible kid, and his legs are long enough to reach the brake and the gas pedal. He has loved cars as long as I can remember, and he knows more about auto mechanics than his dad and I do. He reads every car magazine he can get his hands on, and already has begun saving money for his own car.

Throughout the past year, we've allowed him to pull our cars in and out of the garage and to drive in circles around the block. I'm happy to report there've been no damages to the neighbors' property, the neighbors, or their vehicles.

But please, Lord, steer us through this phase of parenthood with our nerves intact.

I'm also praying for the other new drivers in my son's class— Jason, Andrea, John, to name a few. I've watched these kids grow up since kindergarten, and can even tell you what some of them wore for Halloween two years ago. I want to see them make it to college, unscratched, and one day raise families of their own. I want them to be safe. Is that too much to ask?

Lord, keep these kids out of heart-wrenching newspaper stories. Give them cool heads as they learn how to navigate the expressways, especially this time of year when unpredictable weather and holiday parties make driving twice as hazardous. Help them memorize all the rules of traffic safety and protect them from reckless drivers.

Lord, I'm asking you to help all new drivers respect their limitations as well as the rights of their passengers. Shield them from road rage, intoxicated drivers, empty gas tanks, flat tires and slippery roads.

Give them the wisdom and maturity to respect the privilege of driving a car.

And finally, Lord, grant me the grace to surrender my car keys and give me the courage I will need to sit calmly in the passenger seat while my son takes the wheel. Amen.

The Homecoming Dance

September 21, 2003

From baptism to bar mitzvah, rituals and rites of passage honor the milestones in our lives.

Certain rituals are so closely tied to autumn, in fact, that I can't imagine the season without them. Raking leaves, visiting cider mills, and digging woolens out of storage are just a few. But the annual high-school homecoming dance crowns them all. At our house, as surely as the maples shed yellow leaves on the lawn, this semi-formal event kicks up a whirlwind of activity and emotion.

Some of it is not pretty.

Since I'm the mother of a son, my homecoming rituals do not include shopping for the ultimate evening gown and the perfect shade of nail polish. Admittedly, I miss playing Fairy Godmother to Cinderella, so I live vicariously through other moms who have teen-aged daughters. That's how I've learned that things are different with boys. The angst level, for instance, is much lower in the wardrobe department. Guys don't worry about their hair, and they don't have to obsess over finding a purse to coordinate with a pair of shoes that will be worn only once.

Traditionally, a boy waits until forty-five minutes before the big event to consider whether or not his dress shirt needs to be unearthed from the closet floor. (This is based on the assumption that he owns a dress shirt.) At that point, all hell breaks loose, sending his beleaguered parents in search of an ironing board while the boy hunts down a pair of matching socks. He also waits until the final hour to announce that his good suit has cake frosting on the lapel—a souvenir from the last major event he attended.

Homecoming rituals will test any parent's mettle, but I believe I'm a sturdier person because of them.

Last year, a week before the big dance, we drove Nate to Nordstrom's to shop for a new shirt and tie. Anticipating conflict, I backed off and let him sort through the merchandise with his dad. I tried to keep quiet—until I spotted a handsome gold dress shirt that was perfect for his black suit.

"Look at this one, guys!" I shouted, holding up the prize. On cue, Doug spotted a great tie to go with it. Our sweet son glanced at the ensemble, rolled his eyes, and muttered his new favorite word, "hideous."

Seconds later, Nate's cell phone rang. It was Andrea—a young lady with impeccable fashion sense. Andrea happened to be shopping in the area and would come to his rescue. She would help him find the right shirt.

Well, when the fashionista arrived in the men's department, she immediately chose—you guessed it—the gold shirt. Suddenly this shirt was awesome, and the tie was cool too. (I bit my tongue and reminded myself that God really does look out for parents, and He is everywhere, including Nordstrom's.)

As I type this, the next homecoming dance is a week away. Just as I did last year, and the year before that, I've reminded Nate to ask a date in advance. Once again, I've explained how girls need time to shop for dresses and book hair appointments. And just as he did last year, the kid kept his plans under wraps until he needed advice on ordering a corsage.

As it turns out, Nate's date this year is Andrea, the lovely young lady with good taste in men's shirts. Thinking ahead last week, we bought Nate a new shirt and tie to co-ordinate with her dress. Thank goodness, Andrea approves. Meanwhile, I'm not taking any chances and have dropped off the black suit at the dry cleaner.

This is senior year, after all, and we've finally learned the steps to the homecoming dance.

Thanks for Being There, Fred Rogers

March 1, 2003

"Those of us who are in this world to educate—to care for—young children have a special calling." —Fred Rogers

I took it pretty hard when I heard Fred Rogers died Thursday morning of stomach cancer. It's been ages since I've even glimpsed his show beyond my routine channel surfing, but I felt as if I were saying good-bye to a favorite uncle.

My teen-aged son Nate looked a bit baffled when I told him that Fred Rogers was hanging up his cardigan sweater for good. Hadn't he disappeared down the rabbit hole a long time ago? Mister Rogers, after all, was old news by the time my boy was six and Thomas the Tank Engine had stolen his affection. And although I cut my own teeth on "Captain Kangaroo" several decades earlier, I'm still grateful for every one of the thirty-plus years that "Mister Rogers' Neighborhood" aired on PBS.

"The thing that was special about Mister Rogers was that he always spoke to children with respect," said Fred Nahhat, Kids Club

Producer for Detroit Public Television. "He was a caring and gentle teacher, but we always knew that he was the grown-up and we were his 'neighbors.' He also had the universal appeal of a great teacher, which is something all children need, and PBS allowed him to do that."

Rogers was clean—squeaky clean. Even cynical grown-ups who dismissed his delivery as corny or simplistic agree that his show upheld strong values and genuine human civility—a rarity in a medium that typically promotes high-tech action and premature sexuality.

"I never thought twice about leaving my kid alone to watch Mister Rogers," another middle-aged mom told me. "He was always wonderfully safe."

At the same time, Rogers wasn't afraid to tackle controversial issues such as divorce, multi-culturalism, anger management, or ecology. He came out of retirement last year to deliver a public service announcement for PBS, coaching parents on how to help little ones cope with the anniversary of the September 11 attacks.

Even off camera, he walked the straight and narrow. An ordained Presbyterian minister, he was a vegetarian and strongly committed to recycling. He never smoked or drank, and reputedly swam daily in the nude. He was married to his college sweetheart, Sara Joanne Byrd, for fifty years, and is survived by two sons and two grandsons.

Not long ago, I read a piece in a women's magazine about an older mother who would secretly watch "Mister Rogers' Neighborhood" when her kids were away at college and she felt lonesome. Watching Fred Rogers, she said, was like being wrapped in a security blanket. It made her feel as though she could reach back and steal a sweet slice of childhood innocence. I knew exactly what she meant.

Like other moms of my baby-boomer vintage, I associate Fred Rogers with my child's tender preschool years. Heading out for work,

I'd always manage to deliver my good-bye kisses just as Mister Rogers slipped on his navy canvas shoes and began warbling, "It's a beautiful day in this neighborhood."

A toddler then, Nate would be nestled on the couch next to "Aunt Marian," our part-time caregiver. By the time I had merged into traffic on Woodward Avenue, Mister Rogers' toy trolley was well on its way to the Neighborhood of Make Believe. Nate barely noticed that I'd left.

"Some of us have entrusted Mister Rogers with our preschoolers' hearts and minds," wrote Joyce Millman for Salon.com in 1999. And she was right. Sometimes we got a little too busy and expected Fred Rogers to fill in for us.

I know I owe a debt of gratitude to Mister Rogers. Every weekday—if only for a half hour—this sweet, gentle man reminded my boy that he was worthy of love and capable of loving others. Rogers began the lessons I'm still trying to impart: That doing the right thing is important; that we must honor our place in the world and give something back.

Thanks, Fred Rogers, for all those beautiful days in our neighborhood.

Swamp Hair

August 3, 2003

At some point during parenthood, you learn to appreciate
irony. Recently, for instance, my ungrateful teen-ager complained about the healthy array of organic products I keep
in the shower for family use.

"Why are we using Sap Moss and African Shea Butter on our
hair?" Nate grilled me on the way to the grocery. "Why can't we
buy real shampoo? Why would anyone want their hair to smell like
a swamp?" I quickly launched into my canned lecture on organic
living. I explained how there's nothing more "real" than the green
bounty spun from Mother Nature's loom.

"But I prefer polymers in my shampoo," Nate said.

"You want man-poo," I shot back.

As Nate likes to point out, I am the weirdest person alive. My
preference for botanical products and natural remedies doesn't stop
in the bathroom. I grow my own basil, enjoy the taste of soy milk,

and have been caught slipping granola in the cookie dough. I'll drive out of my way to buy groceries that aren't laced with hormones and antibiotics, or fertilized with sewage sludge. I've been known to ask managers of local markets to carry organic produce, and have even sent thank-you notes to those who've graciously complied.

Of course, I still buy packaged convenience foods, and I don't beat myself up when I don't serve complete vegetarian meals from certified organic produce. And because the guys insist on it, I still stock our bathrooms with deodorant soap and "real" shampoo. Much as I'd like to, I don't have the time or wherewithal to detoxify my entire household, let alone dust the place weekly.

But if an organic product is readily available and affordable, I'll try it. I appreciate and support the farmers who respect my planet and my health.

That said, I realize synthetic chemicals can work miracles and save lives. Covering this topic for another article, I was rightfully reminded by a medical doctor that the word "natural" can be deceiving—and doesn't necessarily mean a product is better. (In his humble opinion, the holistic health movement was "all tofu and hogwash.") But even before Meryl Streep made it cool to buy organic, I had some doubts about the additives in the stuff we consume. I started doing my own research after my son was born, and the more I read, the more I got spooked.

Debra Lynn Dadd, a consumer activist and contributor to *Natural Home* magazine, told me that more than 70,000 chemicals are in use worldwide, with nearly 1,000 new ones added every year. While many of these potions are safe enough for human use, she said, the majority of them have not been fully tested.

Not to panic. The organic way of living is about finding new solutions—and respecting nature—while minding our own health. Maybe someday scientists will discover that polymers are good for us, or that carcinogens are beneficial in the right doses. For all I know, next week some newscaster will announce that the preservatives in our breakfast cereal will cure dementia and motor oil will prevent breast cancer.

For now, I'd like to believe the extra money I spend on certified organic products might buy us a little more time on a cleaner, healthier planet. And that's why I'll keep using Sap Moss shampoo, even if my hair smells like a swamp.

———————————

All My Children

May 9, 2004

When people ask me how many kids I have, I tell them I've lost count.

This might sound strange or irresponsible to most parents, but some of you know exactly what I mean. If, like me, you're the parent of an only child, you've probably invested a lot of time scouting for playmates to foster some pseudo sibling rivalry in your own backyard. To entertain an "only," you often have to play Pied Piper to the neighborhood kids.

But I look back fondly on the years I made our home kid-friendly and child-proof, and I like to think I became a more patient parent while getting to know other people's children. So I like to remind younger moms that it's really worth the effort to host as many playmates as you can. Keeping extra snacks on hand is always a good start. But you also need to lower your standards for house and garden.

One summer, for instance, my son and the neighborhood kids decided to build a fort out of discarded appliance boxes. Combing parking lots and trash piles, they collected enough scrap metal and cardboard to make our entire yard look like a temporary shelter for Royal Oak's homeless population. Occupying our property for weeks, the fort was a tribute to inventive teamwork. Still, I was amazed our neighbors never complained about its lack of curb appeal.

Later, in the middle school years, the kids developed a burning interest in chemistry, often using our home as a laboratory. One example: There was the time my son and a buddy decided to make their own paper pulp in the basement. Using an old ten-speed blender, the two boys pulverized newspaper scraps in a perilous base of water and craft glue. One of them forgot to put the top on the blender, and the resulting glop is still evident on the basement ceiling.

Our home was also frequently chosen as a location for school video projects. I don't recall where the kids obtained all the pyrotechnics they used for special effects, but the final footage was typically awesome. One year, after the crew filmed *Macbeth* for an English literature class, I spent several days picking candle wax from the Oriental carpet in the hallway.

Believe it or not, I'm really going to miss all of this. As the old cliché goes, kids grow up way too fast. By the time you've finally figured out how to spell baccalaureate, they're packing for college and you're praying they'll come back to mess up your house all over again.

Next Sunday I'll be watching the graduation ceremony for Shrine Catholic High School's Class of 2004. There will be tears and accolades and promises to keep in touch. There will be words of gratitude for teachers and school administrators—and for all the parents who created a real extended family for these kids.

Decked in cap and gown, my son will pose for photographs with the talented young people who've graced the past thirteen years of his life. I will add these to our family albums, which are already bursting with earlier photos of the same kids dressed up for field trips, Halloween contests, and homecoming dances.

I've also kept a nostalgic stash of notes from these youngsters. Some are thank-you cards for special gifts or birthday parties. There's even a heartfelt letter of apology for the spilled candle wax from Lady Macbeth. Re-reading these notes never fails to touch me, and I couldn't be more proud.

They say it takes a village to raise a child, and I've never doubted this maxim. But I've also grown to believe it takes a village to raise a mother.

———————

Happy Birthday, Dr. Seuss!

March 1, 1998

It was the late 1950s, and he put the fun back in reading when he booted Dick and Jane out of my neighborhood. To me, he was (and still is) the wizard of words, the "gandorious" great-uncle of terrific tongue-twisters.

To many adults who have since become parents, he's a beloved household icon. His rhymes have thrilled more young bookworms than even he could have imagined. And nobody could imagine things quite like Theodor Seuss Geisel, otherwise known as Dr. Seuss.

His influence is so awesome, in fact, that March 2—Geisel's birthday—is designated "Cat in the Hat Day." Endorsing the holiday, the National Education Association suggests we celebrate by reading to a child tomorrow evening.

Starting in 1937, when he wrote and illustrated his first book, *And to Think That I Saw It on Mulberry Street*, Geisel found his niche churning out tales of the weird and the whimsical, populating them with squawking fish and top-hatted cats. Even today, few other children's authors can tickle a four-year-old funny bone as swiftly as Dr. Seuss. Which is why it's hard to believe that this creator of nerkles and nerds had no kids of his own. Yet he penned forty-seven children's books—and sold more than 100 million copies in more than a dozen languages.

Geisel was born in 1904 in Springfield, Massachusetts. His father was a brewer who ran a zoo during Prohibition—a zoo that undoubtedly provided endless fodder for young Geisel's fantasies. (Geisel, by the way, coined the term "nerd" in *If I Ran the Zoo*.) In 1925 he graduated from Dartmouth, where he'd drawn cartoons for a humor magazine. While studying literature at Oxford in England, he met Helen Palmer, an American literature student who encouraged him to pursue an art career. For a while he drifted in Paris.

In 1927 he came back to the states to marry Helen Palmer. Though he had planned to write novels, the Depression temporarily derailed his art career, and he resumed writing gags for humor magazines. Though his first attempts to publish had been difficult, by the late 1950s "Dr. Seuss" was producing nearly two children's books a year. Delighting young baby boomers and their parents, *Horton Hears a Who* was published in 1954, followed by *How the Grinch Stole Christmas* and *The Cat in the Hat* in 1957.

After Helen Palmer's death in 1967, Geisel married Audrey Dimond and acquired two stepdaughters. He died in 1991 at eighty-seven, with his family at his bedside.

"His contribution was making reading fun again," says Laurie Harris, a Pleasant Ridge parent and series editor of *Biography Today* for young readers. "The rhythm and warmth of his words stay in a child's head forever."

"I like nonsense," Geisel once said. "It wakes up the brain cells. Fantasy is a necessary ingredient in living; it's a way of looking at life through the wrong end of a telescope."

But as every fan discovers, Geisel's "nonsense" isn't just for kids. His stories are laced with sophisticated messages and illuminating parables, which is why they're so much fun to read aloud—with or without children. *The Butter Battle Book*, for example, tackles the perils of the atomic age. Meanwhile, the uproarious Cat in the Hat gets into big trouble, yet somehow manages to redeem himself and straighten out his messes.

Whether we're nine or seventy-nine, after all, there are many horrific hills to climb and, yes, incredible kooks to reckon with.

———————

Kids' Books

March 7, 2004

T here's a bookshelf in my study that might make you question my sanity, if not my age. It's crowded with titles like *Madeline and the Bad Hat, The Polar Express, Green Eggs and Ham, Eloise Goes to Paris, Little Women,* and *Alice's Adventures in Wonderland.*

Some are worn around the edges. Others are brand-new replacements of old favorites I read as a child. Several belonged to my son, now eighteen, who will get them back when he has a home of his own someday.

Nestled around these books are nostalgic toys and dolls, including the infamous Thing One and Thing Two from Dr. Seuss's *The Cat in the Hat.* When I bought my blue-haired "Things" before Christmas last year, I swore I'd give them to my little nephew in New Jersey. But then I changed my mind. I'm not always good about sharing my toys.

My kids' bookshelf has become an altar in the true sense of the word. It pays homage to the stories and characters that made me fall in love with reading. Every time I sit down to work, I'm reminded that literature can inspire kids to overcome challenges, explore new ideas, and even grow up to be writers.

And here's the craziest part: I've never outgrown these books. Sometimes, when I'm feeling stuck or uninspired, I revisit their pages.

> Way out at the end of a tiny little town was an old overgrown garden, and in the garden was an old house, and in the house lived Pippi Longstocking...

So begins my all-time favorite tale by Swedish author Astrid Lindgren.

An only child and hypersensitive, I was at the critical juncture between childhood and early adolescence when a grade-school teacher introduced me to red-haired Pippi. By today's standards Pippi would need Ritalin, but I wanted to be exactly like her.

She was certifiably wacky—the first free spirit I'd encountered. I admired the way she bent rules and colored outside the lines, yet always handled the consequences with charm and tact. Best of all, Pippi lived by herself at Villa Villekulla, managing quite nicely with her own horse and a pet monkey.

> Pippi was indeed a remarkable child. The most re-markable thing about her was that she was so strong. She was so very strong that in the whole wide world there was not a single police officer as strong as she!

My love affair with the printed word has pulled me through some of the toughest times in my life. When I was recovering from hip surgery, for instance, books eased my pain and helped me take flight—even when my legs didn't work. Books helped me heal and grow strong, though I never figured out how to lift a horse like Pippi did.

Last Tuesday was the 100th birthday of Theodor Seuss Geisel, the beloved Dr. Seuss. Since 1998, the National Education Association has used the author's birthday to launch its Reading Across America program. And this month, schools, bookstores and libraries will host numerous activities to get kids excited about reading.

But you don't need a formal program to get started. Round up some kids—your own or a neighbor's—and read your childhood favorites aloud with them. Arrange an impromptu field trip to your local library. Find a character your kids can relate to, and help them learn more about its author.

As Aldous Huxley once wrote, "Everyone who knows how to read has it in their power to magnify themselves, to multiply the ways in which they exist, to make their life full, significant, and interesting."

Books do change lives. And that's worth celebrating any day of the year.

Growing Up In Print

August 15, 2004

I 've been writing this column for nearly ten years now, and still it's hard to believe my son was only nine when I began it.

Back in 1994, *Daily Tribune* Editor Mike Beeson gave me free rein to write a personal column, which is basically a public diary in weekly installments. It's considered a plum assignment by many journalists, yet I'm often conflicted about revealing too much of my home life, especially the parts involving my son.

It's not easy to write about a child without invading his privacy—and I'm guessing that a good family therapist would advise against it. For that reason, I've rarely published Nate's name in the local newspapers, referring to him simply as "my son," which isn't exactly camouflage in a close-knit community.

So I owe Nate a huge debt of gratitude for being such a good sport, most of the time. He was always there to help when I was learning how to use a computer, keeping me on schedule and averting many a deadline crisis. (Thinking ahead, I haven't figured out how I'll handle the inevitable computer crashes and meltdowns when he's no longer living at home.)

When Nate was younger, he didn't always read the paper. But he always knew when he'd been the topic of the week. The column I wrote about the time he left an empty pop can with bees buzzing inside it—under his bed—was a big hit with his grade-school teachers. To my credit, I've avoided truly sensitive issues, including Nate's fourth-grade obsession with "Star Trek," his first girlfriend, and his first fender-bender. And in middle school, there was a temporary dry spell after he'd asked me to stop writing about him and his friends for a while. It was hard for me to honor that request, since readers often told me they liked "the kid columns" best. But I did.

Last week, I ran across an old *Daily Tribune* column from August 6, 1995.

Titled "Don't Worry, Mom," it ran on the weekend I had reluctantly allowed Nate, then nine, to visit a water park in Muskegon with a classmate and his parents. I was apprehensive about the trip because I didn't know the family very well, and Nate hadn't traveled very far without his dad and me. The column, in a nutshell, was about letting go of our kids and allowing them to take the necessary steps toward independence and maturity, which is easier said than done for nearly every parent I've met.

"This is the irony in raising kids," I wrote near the end of the column. "When they are small and tugging on our sleeves, we crave some breathing space. When they are older and backing out of the driveway, we want them to hurry back."

Like most writers, I'm often embarrassed by earlier material. I wish I could go back and tighten things, rework some paragraphs, and make myself sound older and wiser than I was at the time. This "Don't Worry" column was particularly sappy. But despite its maudlin tone, the topic really hit home again.

Later this week, my husband and I will drive Nate down to South

Bend, Indiana, where he'll begin his first year of college. We're all excited—and a little sad, too.

Nine years ago, I somehow understood that Nate's weekend trip to Muskegon was a baby step toward this incredible milestone. And while I haven't totally mastered the art of letting go, this time I've got a better grip on myself.

It helps to know that Nate is fiercely independent and ready for this new adventure. One of the perks of being nearly four hours away, after all, is that his new life on campus won't be easy for me to document in the newspaper.

———————————

Empty Nester

August 29, 2004

"We're all in this together—by ourselves."
—Lily Tomlin

"It will be hard watching her get on that bus for the first time," my friend Jane confided last week. "She's got her new supplies, a Barbie book bag, and the cutest new dress—and she's so excited. I'm the one who isn't ready to let go."

Jane's firstborn starts kindergarten this week, but her sentiments echo those of older parents whose kids are college freshmen. We're struggling to let go too, having delivered our eager sons and daughters to institutions of higher learning all over the state, from the University of Michigan to Hillsdale College. By now, they've unpacked crates of midnight snacks and taped posters to their dormitory walls.

Those kids were in kindergarten 100 years ago. Or was it only yesterday? Today, a few of their parents suddenly bear the dubious title of "empty nester."

I'm writing this piece after depositing Nate on the ivy covered campus of the University of Notre Dame, where everyone did their best to make me feel better about leaving him. There were poignant speeches about the need to give our children "roots and wings." There were student mixers, campus tours, and even a riveting sendoff for tearful parents, accompanied by the marching band.

That was the easy part.

As I told Doug on the long drive home, the biggest challenge, at least for me, will follow in the quiet weeks ahead. While I am concerned about how our son will handle such a vast banquet of opportunity, I believe his time away at college will ultimately mold him into a person of good character. A person who does his own laundry.

Meanwhile, I have to figure out how to get comfortable in our empty nest. I honestly don't want to end up like the deserted mom I read about who found comfort watching "Mister Rogers" reruns.

After eighteen years of bending my career around home and family, I'm just a little uneasy. While I've always thought of myself as a working mom, the emphasis was usually on "mom" and not on "working." Like everyone else who semi-retires from a job, I can't help but wonder: Who the heck am I, now that my role has changed?

A self-employed writer, I can't drive off to an office each morning and bury this question under a familiar stack of paperwork. And I can't hash it out with coworkers at break time. I must shamble around my oddly clean and quiet house, alone with my coffee mug and my deadlines, and confront my identity crisis head on.

"The 'terrible twos' may not have been pleasant, but at least we knew they were coming," write Karen Coburn and Madge Treeger in their helpful handbook, *Letting Go: A Parents' Guide to Understanding the College Years* (Perennial Currents).

"Information and reassurance were readily available if we felt uncertain about our children's development or our roles as parents. But when we send our sons and daughters off to college, there are no Dr. Spocks to reassure us, no guidelines for moving through this time of transition."

Sending a child to college can seem like you're launching him to Jupiter. As I remind my fellow empty nesters, it helps to stay connected to your community. It's the perfect time to jump-start your career, get reacquainted with your spouse, or adopt an abandoned retriever from the local animal shelter.

It also helps to hear a voice on the phone saying, "Hey, Mom, I really like it here. It's going to be a great year! And I need another check for textbooks. "

———————

Social Life

Random Acts of Rudeness

July 24, 2002

I t was early on a Saturday evening, and the fast-food restaurant we'd chosen was nearly empty. Not a good sign.

But my family and I were hungry, and not in the mood to battle for a parking space near the better eateries downtown. So we stayed to order burgers and fries.

A lone teen-ager was stationed behind the cash register, obviously chatting with a friend on his cell phone. We stood in front of Mr. Social for several minutes before he finally glanced our way and mumbled something about taking our order. Still on the phone, the kid used his free hand to punch our selections into the computer. He never made eye contact, and forgot to thank us for stopping by. Miss Manners would call this "fast-food informality"—though I doubt she'd excuse it.

Have good manners gone the way of the manual typewriter?

Drivers run us off the road and shout obscenities. Children who don't get their way throw tantrums in department stores and nice restaurants. Grown-ups chew peas and carrots with their mouths open.

Meanwhile, party-goers are too busy to R.S.V.P., and few recipients can be bothered to write thank-you notes.

Donald McCullough, author of *Say Please, Say Thank You: The Respect We Owe One Another* (Perigee Books) insists we can do better.

Extolling the virtues of not-so-common courtesy, McCullough pleads a strong case for reviving good manners. He's not talking about the "Emily Post etiquette" we drag out for the holidays and quickly stash away with the crystal stemware. Instead, McCullough hopes to salvage the basic human courtesies that help smooth out the rough edges of our daily encounters.

"Our lives are built one small brick at a time, ordinary day by ordinary day," he writes. "With each little expression of thoughtfulness we create something of immense significance—character, both our own and that of others."

McCullough is a pastor and president of San Francisco Theology Seminary, but he's hardly a stuffed shirt in a preacher's robe. His book is funny. Irreverent humor sparkles throughout thirty-six essays covering such topics as the importance of paying what you owe, arriving on time, and not passing wind in public. Even the smallest offense ultimately chips away at our humanity, he says, suggesting that America's boorish lack of manners is partly due to our inflated sense of individual entitlement.

"If something wonderful happens, we hardly pause to give thanks," he says. "We had it coming to us, after all." On the other hand, we feel cheated when things don't go our way. We rant, rave, or point a finger in blame—quite often, the middle finger.

McCullough asks us to imagine how different life would be if everyone started practicing deliberate acts of civility, such as apologizing for mistakes, expressing gratitude, respecting the needs of others, and serving customers with a smile. Glory be!

My own faith was restored last week when I received a note from a teen-ager whose high-school graduation party I'd attended recently. He expressed sincere appreciation for the check I'd written, adding, "But more than getting a check, I was glad to see you at my party." Handwritten on monogrammed stationery, the note was short and sweet—but I couldn't have been more pleasantly surprised.

Address Books

August 15, 1999

Some things will always defy our control. Keeping a kid in the same shoe size for more than six months is one example; maintaining a neat, fully updated address book from one year to the next is another.

I'm talking about the old-fashioned, non-electronic address books that keep us in social contact—the dog-eared pages we've crammed with birthday reminders, letters to answer, and cards announcing new addresses for relocated loved ones.

My own address book is a bit confusing, even to my husband, but it does have a system. For example, one page might be scribbled with little arrows and codes referencing another section of the book ("Look under H/Hill"). This usually means that someone has remarried and changed her name, or that a cousin has left for college or moved to his own apartment.

No matter how badly it's organized, my address book is irreplaceable, especially during emergencies. This hit me seven years ago after my father died. One of the first things my mother and I did was comb through our address books to locate former coworkers, distant cousins, and old friends who needed to be notified of Dad's passing. Each name, each address, was a chapter in my father's history.

Your own address book is probably a chronicle of your ever-evolving relationships—an autobiography in progress. And since relationships are inherently messy, it stands to reason that your address book is messy too. Flipping through mine recently, I made the following observations:

— Reflecting the national average, many of my friends are divorced or working on second marriages.

— Divorce often forces us to choose between friends who used to be a couple.

— Having kids makes a huge difference in our social circle, not to mention the restaurants we frequent.

— The more people we know and love, the harder it is to send birthday cards on time.

— As we age, the line between friends and family starts to blur.

Catching up on the phone last week, Margaret, my former college roommate, and I decided that our midlife definition of "old friends" covers people we've known and loved unconditionally for at least half of our lives. They're the first ones we call when the biopsy results come back or our kids won the big tournament at school.

That's not to say I undervalue the various gifts my newer friends bring to the table. Some are skilled counselors or tireless cheerleaders; others are better at listening than advice-giving. One brings comic relief to every party, while another is the perfect companion for a silent retreat at a monastery. All have expanded my outlook and enriched my life, and I look forward to our future together.

But I've also found that while most of us change or evolve over time, our friendships don't always change or evolve with us. One friend and I drifted so far apart in our interests that we might just as well have moved to opposite sides of the planet. Another disappeared without a trace after a heartrending divorce.

While every relationship has its low points, the stronger ones survive conflict as well as change of address. But I've learned it's never healthy to cling to an alliance that has turned deceitful or draining or destructive. As Emerson said, friendship should offer mutual "aid and comfort" through all of life's passages. I think it should be fun, too.

A few people with whom I've lost touch or parted company are still listed in my address book. At one time, those relationships filled crucial gaps in my life and helped shape the person I am today. I still feel twinges of regret whenever I pause at the pages showing their names and numbers. And because there are a few good memories also attached to those names, I can't quite bring myself to erase them.

Girl Groups

May 30, 2004

"There was a definite process by which one made people into friends, and it involved talking to them and listening to them for hours at a time."   —Dame Rebecca West

Nothing beats the power of a girl group. Whether you're swamped with a crisis at work, unruly kids, or too much estrogen, you can always count on the harmony of other women's voices to lift you higher.

Girl groups rock. And I don't mean the musical variety, although I'm a fan of those too. But right now I'm applauding the whole idea of women banding together to form their own circles and support groups. Never in the history of womankind have we been so overbooked, so stressed, and so starved for emotional connection as we are today. Like the quilting circles of my grandmother's era, female support groups can keep a gal from unraveling at the seams and help repair the snags in the crazy patchwork of her workaday life.

But first, some definitions are in order. A support group should never be confused with a clique, which still has the hollow ring of adolescence. *Webster's New World College Dictionary* defines a clique as "a small, exclusive circle of people; a snobbish or narrow coterie."

A support group, on the other hand, has a large collective heart. It is typically formed around a positive agenda—to explore complex issues like new motherhood or breast cancer, for example. Individuality is welcomed and encouraged, and useful information is exchanged to aid the group as a whole. The conversation is always therapeutic.

Over the years I've belonged to several women's clubs, but the women's spirituality group I helped form at my church is the one I've needed most. This incredible family of women has coached me through major surgery, mild depression, career dilemmas, a spiritual crisis, my son's graduation, and midlife hormonal shifts.

Meeting monthly for several years, we've all rehashed a variety of topics, including healing and forgiveness, letting go of our kids, rebuilding friendships, caring for aging parents, and caring for our stressed-out souls. A few in the group have lost children and husbands, converted from different faiths, and battled serious health crises.

Taking a quick glance around our circle, you'd agree that we're an uncommon grab bag of gals. Our ages range from forty-four to eighty-four, and we represent a wide variety of professions from social work to finance. The main things we have in common, as one member says, are one another's trust and our faith. And love.

"The older women teach me about the next stages of life, as well as how to handle spiritual challenges," a younger member explains. "They help me tackle my problems with more strength. I'm awed by these women."

I can't imagine coping without them, either. Working at home, I'm isolated most of the day. As much as I enjoy writing, I tend to live inside my head and get the blues easily. Thankfully, meetings with my women's group seem to fall at exactly the right times—when my own jumbled patchwork of a life could use a little mending and some social contact.

If you're inspired to form your own official girl group, here's what to do.

Decide on a focus for your meetings. Keep the circle small, preferably under twelve women. If it's much larger, there won't be time for everyone to get a word in edgewise. For tips on how to rotate leadership and discussions, consult *The Millionth Circle: How to Change Ourselves and the World—The Essential Guide to Women's Circles*, by Jean Shinoda Bolen. Commit to a regular meeting time at the same location, unless you prefer to rotate your gatherings at various homes. For everyone's sanity, keep the refreshments light, as in coffee or tea and store-bought cookies.

Above all, your support group should be about nourishing friendships and feeding the soul. So, forget the gourmet brownies but be sure to bring an open heart.

The Old Neighborhood

June 8, 2003

It had been a little while since we'd been together. But despite the unseasonably cool weather for June, the talk was as warm and familiar as the coffee cupped in my hands. This time, we were celebrating the high-school graduation of one of our kids.

It struck me, as I glanced around the room, that no matter how much time passes or how far away I move in the future, these folks will always feel like home to me.

They are my old neighbors.

My family and I moved a few blocks south of their enclave a while ago. And as much as we enjoy the neighborhood we live in now, I have to admit I left part of my heart, not to mention a spectacular lilac bush, in our former backyard.

I was pregnant with Nate when Doug and I moved there eighteen years ago. Obsessive new homeowners that we were, we spent our free time renovating and decorating. It wasn't until Nate needed playmates that we started connecting with other families on the block. As another mom told me, children turn your street into a neighborhood.

Unfortunately, that street was a shortcut to Woodward, one of the busiest thoroughfares in Oakland County, and too many drivers were oblivious to our residential speed limit. It wasn't unusual to spot carloads of teen-agers (or clueless adults) speeding past our house en route to the drag strip at the end of our block. And how could I forget the inebriated savage who stumbled out of a car and relieved his bladder on the new pine tree I'd just planted next to our driveway?

Naturally, we wanted to protect our kids as well as the peace of our carefully groomed street. So we banded together—about a dozen of us—to devise a plan. We would storm City Hall and demand that our officials close our street. My husband, the resident architect, drew up plans for diverting traffic. All of us took turns hosting civic meetings in our homes, not realizing at the time that we were actually cementing a lifelong friendship.

Of course, the city had no intention of redesigning our street. As a token gesture of compromise, we were given stop signs, which mysteriously disappeared a few years later. But our "town hall" meetings didn't stop. Instead, they morphed into coffee hours and block parties and semi-annual dinner outings.

You hear a lot of talk about community these days—why it's not as easy to cultivate and what we can do about it. Blaming our corporate work ethic and the time we spend on the Internet, sociologists claim that neighborly activities like pot-lucks and plant exchanges are remnants of the Victorian age.

Not so, in my experience. My family and I learned the secrets of community building in our early years as homeowners, thanks to a handful of neighbors who cared about something bigger than their own backyards.

Today, the little ones we were trying to protect from traffic are licensed drivers. Some, like the one whose graduation party I attended last week, are leaving for college in the fall. But they all seem to appreciate the friendships that grew around them years ago, and they promise to keep coming back to celebrate.

Stress-free Dinner Parties

November 10, 2002

"A smiling face is half the meal." —Latvian proverb

M y friend Pam knows the real secret of successful entertaining, and I wish I could be more like her.

Pam doesn't spend weeks obsessing over what she'll serve for dinner, nor does she turn her life inside-out when a carload of company arrives from Cincinnati for the weekend. And it's not that she doesn't care. Pam and her husband, Steve, genuinely enjoy hosting friends and family, which partly explains how they make it look so effortless.

I like to remember the winter evening my husband and I were invited to their home for an impromptu dinner with another couple.

"Wear something comfy, and don't expect anything fancy," Pam warned us. "We're just having a casual meal before the holiday rush." But that didn't mean beer and pizza on paper plates. This was a real celebration of friendship.

Pam had dressed her table with a navy blue cloth and a simple homemade centerpiece of apples, tangerines, and pears. Around the fruit she lit a few votive candles. Before lifting a fork or a wine glass, Pam asked that we all join hands and give thanks for our years of friendship and the chance to slow down long enough to eat a meal together.

As promised, for dinner she served comfort food, including roast pork, a vegetable casserole, and spicy baked apples for dessert. The whole evening, in fact, was cozy and relaxed and nourishing—and Pam insisted she enjoyed it all as much as we did.

"We wouldn't entertain as often if we felt we had to make a big deal out of it," she told me.

I'm still trying to break the habit of making "a big deal" out of hosting company. The folks we typically entertain, after all, don't expect a major production. But like many women I know, I was brainwashed into thinking that making dinner for company is synonymous with staging a photo shoot for a shelter magazine. I worry that my guests will scrutinize my housekeeping and discover my inner slob. And while I love to cook, I still worry that anything I serve, whether it's meatloaf or Lobster Newberg, won't turn out like the photos in the cookbook.

Of course, my feelings of culinary insecurity always rise like bread dough at holiday time. Come fall, even before I've folded up the Halloween ghosts, I'm already fretting about Christmas decorations and turkey recipes. By mid November, everything on my to-do list starts leaping around in my head like a chorus of nervous elves. And by the time the holidays are over, I'm thanking heaven that *they are OVER.*

But it doesn't have to be like this. Fussy entertaining puts everyone on edge and creates just as much pressure for guests as it does for the host.

The quickest way back to sanity is to remind ourselves that most people are easily pleased with home cooking and real conversation.

We don't have to own Waterford crystal or serve meals worthy of a four-star chef. And the ones who truly enjoy our company aren't judging us by our napkin rings.

Sharing an evening with good friends is a gift in itself when the occasion is heartfelt, the presentation simple. Pam and Steve figured this out a long time ago, and that's why it's always such a pleasure to gather at their table.

Black Holes

July 31, 2002

A full-time mother of three told me she looks forward all year to summer break and hates to see it end. Is she nuts? Does she really enjoy refereeing troops of rowdy kids in her basement and making dozens of grape jelly sandwiches on short order?

"I love summer because I get a reprieve from the back-stabbing at school bake sales and Mothers' League meetings," my friend explains. "And I don't have to deal with the WWDLM."

The WWDLM?

"That's shorthand," she says, "for the 'Woman Who Doesn't Like Me' at school."

Even if you've never been a homeroom mom, you know exactly what she means. You've got your own social nemesis.

The woman who doesn't like you might be the tetchy neighbor who never fails to criticize your kids. Or the toxic relative who snubs you at family barbecues. Or maybe she's the caustic co-worker who nixes every bright idea you bring to weekly office meetings. No matter what you say or do, you'll never win these people over. Even when you're as sweet as key lime pie, they'll refuse to sit at the table of your friendship.

Sue Patton Thoele calls them "the black holes" in our personal universe.

Author of *A Woman's Book of Soul: Meditations for Courage, Independence & Spirit* (Conari Press), Thoele recalls an awkward time when she wasn't hitting it off with two women in her own social circle.

"The energy I put out to these women was merely absorbed as if it had disappeared into a black hole and none came back to me," she explains. As a psychotherapist, Thoele understood that we all tend to project our unconscious feelings onto other people. She knew that the qualities we dislike in others are often the same ones we unwittingly dislike in ourselves. But then the simple truth finally dawned: The cold-shouldered women in her circle were lousy candidates for friendship.

"If we're saddled with the belief that everyone needs to like us in order for us to be acceptable—or that we should be able to be friends with anyone—we cause ourselves a lot of pain," she explains. "We're simply 'energetic misses' with some people."

Like Thoele, I've spent years trying to figure out why some relationships fly while others can't seem to get off the ground.

And I'm still in awe of the fact that men rarely waste time wondering why some people don't like them. They shake hands and move on. Women, however, tend to lose sleep devising ways to appease or impress folks who needn't count so much. We work hard to avoid conflict and maintain the status quo, often at our own expense.

But healthy relationship are reciprocal—a graceful dance of give-and-take. So when we find ourselves stumbling into "Black Hole Territory," as Thoele says, it's best to trust our intuition and bow out.

Not everyone, after all, has to uphold our political beliefs or religious convictions. Not everyone has to share our taste in books and movies. Other people have every right to dislike us, our kids, and our carrot cake recipes. And as long as we remain civil, we're entitled to reciprocate the feeling.

Seven Reasons to Screen Your Calls

March 8, 1998

"In Hell all the messages you ever left on answering machines will be played back to you."
— Judy Horacek, cartoonist

This Tuesday is Alexander Graham Bell Day—the anniversary of the telephone's invention.

To recap your history lessons: On March 10, 1876, Bell made the famous first connection when he spilled acid on himself in a Boston laboratory and called to his assistant, "Mr. Watson, come here." Working in the next room, Watson heard Bell's words on an apparatus they'd been tinkering with, and telephones have been ringing ever since.

Like others who work from home, I owe a debt of gratitude to Mr. Bell. The telephone is my lifeline. Phone wires connect me to editors, doctors, friends and family, not to mention the Internet. It wards off loneliness.

But convenience has a price. Mr. Bell didn't realize on that fateful March afternoon that his invention would be as intrusive as it was miraculous. And that's why I'm just as grateful for answering machines.

There's a fine line between people who screen superfluous calls and the ones who avoid them entirely. I'm often in the latter category. If I'm too tired to chat, I duck behind my answering machine and pretend I'm not home. Sometimes I send e-mail and think I'm off the hook.

Of course, I'm not fooling everybody. A few of my friends typically begin their phone messages with, "I know you're really there, listening, so I'll make this short."

Some people think it's rude or arrogant to ignore a ringing phone, but my phone avoidance is nothing personal. It's a defense mechanism. I literally tune out the ringing to save my sanity—and I know I'm not the only one who does.

"I hate wasting time on the phone," admits my friend Pam, who prefers to talk in person over lunch.

These days most of us are incredibly over-connected. Our ever-widening circles are populated with dozens of people, many of whom expect our immediate attention at the very moment they decide to make contact. We're so busy fielding messages, from e-mail to faxes to Federal Express, that one more call can easily push us over the edge. Screening calls at home is a way to steal a moment of privacy from our wired world.

But there is such a thing as phone etiquette. Eventually, spurned callers catch up with us, and they usually want to know where we've been and why they've been ignored.

With that in mind, I present the Seven Tactful Excuses of Highly Effective Screeners. Think of these as your permission slip to lean back, uncork your merlot, and toast Mr. Bell's anniversary while you let the answering machine make your apologies.

1. You're expecting an important call. It could be news from the hospital. An answer from your agent. Or your child's pediatri-

cian. This isn't the time to tie up the line with miscellaneous chit-chat. You can talk to Aunt Beth later.

2. You're in the bathroom. There's absolutely no need to apologize for not answering the phone if you've been tending to personal hygiene or nursing a case of intestinal flu. Later, if the caller demands an explanation, he or she deserves to hear all the details you're willing to rehash.

3. You are dodging telemarketers. Enough said.

4. You've already logged more than an hour on the phone—first with the boss, then with a colleague. If you spend the rest of the day listening to your mother complain about her taxes, you'll miss a deadline and, ultimately, a paycheck.

5. You're napping and don't even *hear* the phone ring. Flawless.

6. Dinner is in progress, in the oven or on the table. Never let a phone conversation spoil your soufflé. Family mealtime is sacred, so unless you're expecting an urgent call, switch on the answering machine. And never leave the table to find out who phoned.

7. You're spending a rare, romantic evening with your spouse. The candles are flickering, the music is playing…and the phone is ringing. Are you going to let that window salesman spoil it again?

Talking Feather

L ike many of the items at the Leaping Lizard gift shop in Traverse City, the talking feather was steeped in Native American lore. As soon as I saw it, I knew it would be the perfect souvenir of my last visit to Northern Michigan.

A bargain at $11.95, the feather was trimmed with strands of tiny multi-colored beads and gracefully suspended from a thin leather cord. But the legend printed on the attached card cinched my decision to buy it: "When crowds gathered and conversation grew louder, it was hard to hear one speaker, so the person wishing to address the crowd was passed 'the talking feather.' It was held above the crowd to signify that the person had the floor as speaker."

I'm not an expert on Native Americana, so I can't vouch for the authenticity of the legend. Regardless, many intriguing possibilities come to mind.

The talking feather would come in handy at our extended family gatherings, especially during the holidays, when several conversations are carried on simultaneously and in competition with televised football games. But what if we all sat down to dinner with the sacred talking feather? Every in-law would be entitled to speak her piece while the rest of the family would listen intently, the room hushed.

Maybe I could use a talking feather to control the flow of conversation between members of my immediate family at our regular dinner hour. The magic words, "Please pass the talking feather," would make our discussions more democratic. Everyone could get a word in edgewise. There would be fewer interruptions and better digestion.

Imagine how different things would be if every American used a talking feather. There would be time to cool our emotions before setting them free. We'd air political opinions more carefully and breathe between sentences.

In the classroom, a teacher could silence a roomful of chatty second graders with a mere wave of a feather.

And what a boon it would be at business meetings when too many chiefs are present. Problems would be solved with greater efficiency, abrasive personalities subdued. Shouting matches would be curtailed, empathy encouraged. The simple phrase, "Please pass the talking feather," would instill a sense of corporate dignity. And should hogging the talking feather become a problem, it could be remedied tactfully: "Excuse me, sir, but how long have you been holding the talking feather?"

A born talker, I'm inclined to interrupt, and sometimes I let my thoughts rush out of my mouth like too much salt from a shaker. I often find myself wishing I could take back the foolish things I've said. But what if I carried the talking feather in my purse, or hung it around my neck, to remind myself to think before speaking?

"The right word may be effective," Mark Twain once said, "but no word was ever as effective as a rightly timed pause."

I'll bet he knew about the talking feather.

———————————

The Gift of Receiving

S everal years ago, when I was diagnosed with osteoarthritis in both hips, I read everything I could find about coping with chronic illness. I was amazed at how often I'd stumble on a paragraph that advised patients to "look for the gift in your pain."

Pain is a gift? Thanks, but no thanks, I'd mutter to myself.

I had just turned forty-four and hadn't planned on slowing down so soon. I still had miles to go with my journalism career and a family that included a very active teen-ager. If pain was my gift, well, where was the return policy?

Within a year of my diagnosis, the disease progressed so quickly that total hip replacement surgery was my only option. By that time, I was unable to walk without assistive devices. Even on a good day, it hurt so much to crawl out of bed that I refused to unplug my heating pad and leave the house. Suddenly I was disabled—and even qualified for a "handicapped" parking permit.

Having been fit and active most of my adult life, I was way too proud to let others watch me struggle on a walker. I hated to appear needy. I started canceling my lunch dates and appointments, and tried to hide behind a steely mask of self-sufficiency.

But my closest friends and family members didn't buy any of it. And it was through their patience and love that I finally discovered the "gift" in chronic illness: It slowly unravels your pride and opens you to the boundless generosity of other people.

"Surrender is no small feat in a culture that applauds the strong, the independent, and the self-sufficient," writes Victoria Moran in *Creating A Charmed Life: Sensible Spiritual Secrets Every Busy Woman Should Know* (HarperSanFrancisco). "That heroic stuff is fine when the problem is something we can handle through our own self-sufficiency. But nobody climbs a mountain alone."

Of course, stubborn self-reliance isn't the sole province of the disabled.

Most women I know pride themselves on being nurturers, fixers, problem-solvers, *givers*. We'll supply all the brownies for the bake sale at school after we've organized the rummage sale at church. We'll rearrange our schedules to baby-sit other people's kids. Just ask, and we'll triple our workload at the office and still make it to the evening PTA meeting. Yet some of us would rather have a wisdom tooth pulled than ask somebody else for a favor when we need it. As a girlfriend told me recently, "It's my job to be the glue that holds everyone and everything together. I can't ask for help."

The truth is, people who care about us really do want to help—if only we'd drop the mask of total self-sufficiency and admit that we're not all-powerful *all* the time.

Discussing the aftermath of September 11 and the clean-up at Ground Zero, a talk show host suggested that if anything positive rose from the ashes of the tragedy, it was that America quickly evolved from a "Me" nation into a "We" nation. As she explained it, even the most self-absorbed among us realized that we cannot function as individual islands. We *need* each other. It was a good lesson for me to review so soon after my first hip replacement surgery. Strapped to a hospital bed and hooked up to several tubes, I was hit with the sobering reality that I wasn't going anywhere by myself.

And during the early weeks of my recovery, I had no choice but to graciously accept support from my family and friends. When my husband processed mountains of laundry at home, I tried not to feel guilty. When our neighbors sent casseroles or offered to drive my carpool shift to school, I swallowed my pride and allowed their care to work like a healing balm. And it did.

As hard as it was to surrender, I discovered there's real strength in vulnerability.

Deep down, I still believe it's more blessed to give than to receive. And I still believe that putting the needs of others first isn't such a bad precept to live by—unless it renders you incapable of accepting a favor or asking for help when you really need it.

Nobody climbs her mountain alone.

Kitchen Duty

Baghdad and Banana Bread

April 23, 2003

"Nothing feeds the center so much as creative work,
even humble kinds like cooking and sewing."
—Anne Morrow Lindbergh

It's probably safe to assume that daily news coverage of combat casualties, weapons of mass destruction, and a skittish economy are making you nervous. These days, all of us are looking for reassurance and comfort.

One friend calms down reading poetry and listening to Ella Fitzgerald CDs, while another does laps at an indoor pool. But once the bombs starting falling on Baghdad earlier this month, I did the first thing I could think of to cheer myself up: I started baking banana bread.

Nobody is more amazed at this than I am.

I came of age in the 1970s, when most of my peers viewed kitchen work as women's enslavement and thought that dinner was just another word for Chinese carry-out. If a social occasion called for brownies or a birthday cake, my girlfriends and I would drive to the nearest grocer and grab what was left on the bakery shelves. Anything remotely domestic, even owning a bread machine, was viewed as a covert affront to the feminist movement.

Fortunately, my attitude toward food preparation changed after my son was born and I started working from home. This change of heart had less to do with my son's preference for homemade cookies and more to do with the fact that working in the kitchen was a creative release from parenting and writing deadlines. Recipes were easier to manage than a cranky three-year-old or an unruly paragraph. Sifting flour and breaking eggs seemed soothing, almost Zen-like.

Before long, I found myself collecting cookbooks, old and new, at garage sales and used book stores. I started reading food essays at bedtime, and soon fell in love with the tools of the craft—wire whisks, imported knives, beautiful glass mixing bowls. I collected aromatic herbs and spices and learned how to use them. And over time I grew to respect the mystical, nurturing powers of homemade food.

But cooking or baking isn't necessarily something I do to nourish others at my table, or to satisfy my own cravings. I'm fed as much by the process as I am by the outcome.

Working in the kitchen, I am in communion with other cooks who've stirred these same ingredients in the past. A whiff of vanilla, for instance, triggers memories of making Christmas cookies with my mother. Kneading dough for scones, I remember baking with my Scottish grandmother, whose strong, freckled arms were always covered in flour. Straining chicken broth, I'm transported back to childhood and the Old World kitchen of a Ukrainian neighbor. The recipes in my batter-stained book reconnect me to previous holidays, picnics, parties, and potlucks. Good times.

"It seems to me that our three basic needs, for food, security, and love, are so entwined that we cannot think of one without the other," wrote food columnist and author, M. F. K. Fisher.

Which is why, when the war in the Middle East broke out and I felt insecure and panicky, my first impulse was to warm the oven and make my favorite banana bread from scratch. As soon as the loaves cooled, I wrapped each one as a gift and delivered them to my neighbors.

———————————

The Child In My Kitchen Isn't Julia

November 1995

I never put stock in the old notion that a kitchen is the sole province of girls and women. As long as they're tall enough to reach the back burners on the stove, our sons can learn to be excellent cooks. The culinary arts have all the right ingredients for little boys. For starters, there's a wide array of fascinating gadgets to play with, not to mention the delicious alchemy of making a mess.

Thanks to the Cub Scouts, my school-age son has acquired some handy new kitchen skills. To earn his Family Member badge last fall, Nate had to complete the following requirements as described in his official Webelo handbook:

"Help plan the meals for your family for at least one week. Help buy the food. Prepare at least three meals for the family."

With Thanksgiving just three weeks away, it seemed the ideal time to introduce my boy to the bounty of our local produce markets. Fortifying my appetite for adventure, I bought him a cookbook that promised to simplify "workday meal preparation." After we agreed on a week's worth of kid-friendly menus, including one for pan-broiled flank steak, I discovered we didn't own most of the book's required "pantry staples." So off we drove to a nearby supermarket—a store with aisles wide enough to accommodate a Cub Scout on a mission with a runaway grocery cart.

I would have preferred a more leisurely pace, but Nate zoomed ahead like a game-show contestant on a three-minute shopping spree.

At the produce aisle, I stopped him long enough to explain how to select a good head of garlic. Then we whirled through the canned-goods section, and over to the spices. As I read the list of ingredients for his recipes, Nate pulled each item from the shelf and hurled it like a missile into the cart. A bottle of curry powder bounced off my bag of lemons, denting a can of stewed tomatoes on the rebound.

Our next stop: the meat counter. After delivering a short lecture on choosing a healthy cut of meat, I asked Nate which of two flank steaks looked the best. Young James Beard opted for the cheapest one. It wasn't until I unloaded our cart in the checkout line that I noticed he'd also chosen a package of gooey Choco-licious cupcakes for dessert. This was *his* menu, of course, so I let it pass.

Back home in the kitchen, I held my breath and let my budding chef do most of the work. With gusto, he pounded three cloves of garlic (only one hit the wall on the other side of the room) then tossed them into the skillet. The hardest part was watching him attack a ripe tomato with a butcher knife. I bit my lip and reminded myself that our freshly painted walls could be hosed down later. The culinary arts, after all, can't be perfected without a few well-intended splatters.

"I don't know why you complain about cooking dinner, Mom— it's really *fun*," Nate said as he seized a spatula and swirled the contents of another saucepan. I grinned at his enthusiasm, never once mentioning the errant globs of rice sliding down the stove.

Served by candlelight, Nate's pan-broiled steak was a remarkable success—and amazingly tender for such a bargain. I whispered a quick prayer of thanks for the Boy Scouts of America, who were providing a terrific service for busy families of tomorrow. Though my Cub didn't quite realize it yet, he'd learned how to prepare the most nurturing gift anyone could offer—the gift of a homemade meal.

Since then, Nate hasn't lost his interest in kitchen work.

"Why don't you rest while I make us some peanut butter sandwiches for dinner," he offered last week. *Bon appetit!*

———————

Just My Cuppa Tea

January 31, 1999

L ately I've noticed a lot of magazine articles touting the wonders of tea, but I don't need to be persuaded. While I still
rely on strong black coffee for my morning jump-start, I'm
primed for the pleasures of tea by the time my workday winds down.

Unlike coffee (tea's rich but nerve-racking cousin), tea is a soul-
soother. Whether you prefer the delicate jasmine aroma of Earl Grey,
or the spicy citrus bouquet of Constant Comment, one cup is enough
to transform the dismal hour between four and five o'clock into an
uplifting occasion.

I can't pour a teapot without remembering my paternal grandmother, Robina Scott, who spent her childhood in rural Scotland,
then immigrated to this country in the 1920s. A lifelong tea drinker,
Grandma Ruby taught me the grown-up custom of "taking tea" when
I was a child.

To a five-year-old whose parents drank coffee, tea rituals seemed
wonderfully prim and sometimes a little exotic. According to Ruby's

native Orkney Island folklore, reading tea leaves was a reliable way to forecast a person's future. Following old-country custom, she would interpret the various shapes of leaves left in a cup, then predict weather conditions, the health of an ailing relative, the sex of an unborn child, or even the arrival of a love letter.

But my grandmother never took fortune-telling seriously, nor was she a British purist who insisted on using loose tea in a metal infuser or strainer. At my urging, in fact, she'd generously stock her kitchen canister with Red Rose tea bags after I had pilfered all the collectible dinosaur cards from the box.

As surely as I can spell brontosaurus, I can still picture the floral-print housedresses Ruby would wear when she "put the kettle to boil" and rolled great masses of dough for her perfect apple pies. During my weekend visits, I was always allowed to make my own cinnamon-sugar strips from her leftover pie dough.

"Use a bit less o' the sugar, dearie," Ruby would scold. "And don't eat the dough before it's done!"

While the pies baked, Ruby and I sat at her kitchen table, dipping and steeping our tea bags until the water in our steaming cups turned amber. Sometimes we talked between sips; mostly we stared quietly out the kitchen window and watched the sparrows, our silver spoons breaking the reverie as they chimed against cup and saucer.

As my grandmother liked to remind me, tea had Oriental origins but was a British import to the early American colonies. As most of us recall from our grade-school history classes, it was heavily taxed by the monarchy and eventually incited the boisterous Boston Tea Party of 1773. Since then, our country has harbored a stubborn preference for coffee.

A mug of coffee is quick, feisty, and all-American—easy to consume on the run in disposable cups.

Tea, on the other hand, requires that we sit down long enough to assemble its various accoutrements. Drinking tea entails a fussy battery of saucers, spoons, bags, lemon wedges, and pots with lids, not to mention the optional milk, honey, or sugar. Which is why most waiters don't cater to tea drinkers; they think we're a high-maintenance bunch and would rather not be bothered with our hot-water refills.

But there's another revolution brewing here. Researchers claim that tea, especially green tea, is naturally laden with antioxidant properties that promote good health. A recent survey conducted by The Tea Council in Great Britain reported that drinking four or five cups of tea per day "may have a beneficial effect on high blood cholesterol and high blood pressure," and may reduce the incidence of certain cancers.

If Ruby were alive today, I doubt these new-age health claims would have impressed her. The real merits of tea, as we both discovered years ago, are tied to its soothing, soul-filling rituals.

An Ode to *Joy*

March 16, 1997

E very cook, no matter how accomplished, relies on a favorite cookbook. Mine is *The Joy of Cooking*, a household staple as dependable as bread and milk.

My copy was a wedding present from an old friend of my mother's. Opening it at my first bridal shower, I had no idea that the book would play a fundamental role in future family celebrations. I piled it carelessly under my stash of recently unwrapped kitchen towels and cooking equipment, and probably didn't express near enough appreciation to the giver.

Yellowed and splashed with seventeen years' worth of stains, it now occupies a shelf with more than thirty other cookbooks, a few of which are souvenirs from my travels. But like an old best friend, *The Joy of Cooking* is the one I turn to first.

The culinary classic was first printed privately by Irma Rombauer in 1931.

"Mrs. Rombauer is to food what Spock is to babies. You can't run a kitchen or bring up an infant without them," observed Laurie Colwin, the late novelist and food columnist. Over the years it has been revised and refined, earning its status as "the one indispensable cookbook." In an era of celebrity chefs and domestic divas, *Joy* proves over and over again that basic is best.

But my 1980 edition is more than a faithful kitchen companion. Thumbing through its pages recently, I realized the book has become a treasured chronicle of my culinary history. It has followed me to four different kitchens, seeing me through countless dinner parties, family feasts, and just-plain-ordinary meals.

The chapter titled "Entertaining," for example, is permanently wrinkled from overuse. Though my mother had tried to instruct me on the art of setting a table when I was younger, I hadn't paid attention. (I'm still confused about the proper placement of bread plates.) And so, when my husband and I started entertaining in the cramped dining nook of our first apartment, I often turned to pages eighteen and nineteen, which illustrate the variations of socially correct table settings.

The "Shellfish" section always evokes memories of New Year's Eve, particularly the first one my husband and I celebrated as newlyweds. Inspired by a scene in a Woody Allen movie, I decided to cook live lobsters, using the directions on page 386. Later on, we established a new tradition of spending New Year's Eve with our longtime friends Laurie and Dan, both of whom share the belief that every year should be begin with fabulous food. Over time, *Joy of Cooking* has provided unforgettable recipes for many of those feasts—including the most impressive Beef Wellington we've ever sampled.

There were a few lean years when *Joy* collected dust on the kitchen shelf. Taking care of a new infant, I had little time or energy left for anything but warming baby formula. Meanwhile, Doug and I survived on pizza and other carry-out cuisine. But I didn't completely neglect my old pal, my favorite cookbook. Even in the late

1980s, *Joy* survived my post-hippie fascination with vegetarian diets. (I still turned to it then for terrific dessert recipes, including the one for Brandied Peaches on page 846.)

Eventually tiring of fried tofu and wild rice, Doug and I happily brought meat and poultry back to the dinner table. Last week, for instance, we bought several pounds of spareribs, which neither of us had ever attempted to prepare at home.

"Should you boil spareribs before grilling them, or what?" asked Doug, who only recently expressed a serious interest in cooking. Before I could take a guess, he was on his way over to the bookshelf. I was impressed, but not at all surprised, that he knew exactly which cookbook to consult. Turning to page 481 in *Joy*, he rolled up his sleeves, filled the kettle, pre-heated the grill, and got to work.

And the spareribs, by the way, tasted just right.

Shortbread and a New Year

December 27, 2001

"We'll tak a cup o' kindness yet,
For auld lang syne." —Robert Burns

It's our turn to host our friends Laurie and Dan for our annual New Year's Eve party, which means it's also time to buy butter and sugar to make authentic Scottish shortbread. It's all part of a folksy tradition that I'll explain further along.

None of us can remember who hosted our first New Year's Eve dinner together—Laurie and Dan, or Doug and I—but the idea was sparked by our frustration with crowded restaurants and inflated holiday prices. Younger and thinner then, we discovered it was just as much fun to cook at home, where we could almost afford to pull out all the stops. Over the years we've experimented with every festive recipe we could pilfer from a cookbook, from Beef Wellington to Creme Brulee. And aside from a few minor culinary disasters, we've always made wonderful memories.

But I should explain the shortbread and the ancient Scottish custom of first footing.

In Scotland, New Year is called Hogmanay, which comes from the old Gaelic term for "new morning." As tradition dictates, your new year will be more prosperous if, at the strike of midnight, a tall, dark stranger walks through your door with a cake or a lump of coal for the fire. In exchange for this good fortune, you must offer the stranger food, ale, wine, or a "wee dram" of whiskey. In some Scottish households today, the offering of choice is shortbread, and it's usually baked in the shape of a sun to symbolize warmth and hospitality for the coming year.

On the other hand—and you'll want to remember this—some individuals bring misfortune if they're the first to cross your threshold as the year begins. A fair-haired man, an undertaker, or a woman, are all considered bad omens. (According to historians, the ancient fear of blond strangers was linked to the memory of the Vikings who pillaged Scotland from the fourth to twelfth centuries.)

Boasting a bit of Scottish blood himself, Dan introduced first footing to our party several years ago, surprising us with shortbread for our New Year's Eve dessert. Following tradition to the letter, he carried his homemade offering through the front door at midnight.

First footing is now part of our annual festivities, although the person who hosts the party usually bakes the shortbread. And things are getting a bit more complicated now that the guys are turning gray and no longer qualify as "tall, dark strangers."

This year, Doug will bake the shortbread for our first footing, and I'll let you know how our luck runs next year after he carries it through the front door. In any event, here's the recipe he uses:

Scottish shortbread

1 cup butter

2 cups sifted all-purpose flour

1/2 cup confectioners' sugar

1/4 teaspoon salt

Preheat oven to 325. Sift together flour, sugar and salt. Blend in butter. (Some cookbooks suggest using a blender; my own Scottish grandma used a fork). Pat stiff dough into an ungreased 9 x 9-inch pan; press the edges. Pierce dough with a fork every inch or so. Bake 25 to 30 minutes. Cut into desired shapes while dough is warm.

No matter where you celebrate—at home or in your favorite restaurant—a new year ought to begin with good food and dear friends.

———————

Martha, Martha, Martha!

March 14, 2004

There she is on the March 15 cover of *Newsweek*, hair askew, frightfully haggard. The caption reads: "COOKED." This is not the sort of publicity that helps sell porcelain dinnerware, wicker laundry baskets, or 250 thread-count sheets.

This is definitely not a good thing.

Martha Stewart, the woman we've loved to parody (and hate), is in deep trouble. And I'm feeling a little sorry for her.

For one thing, as Allan Sloan pointed out in a recent *Newsweek* column, Martha's mistakes are, in his opinion, "stupidity, greed and cluelessness...not criminal offenses." He makes a good point, especially when you recall the list of athletes, politicians, and celebrities who've done much worse than mess with a few stocks, yet are running around scot-free. There are much bigger fish than Martha to deep fry.

But I'll admit it took me a while to warm up to Martha. For

starters, her icy perfectionism was a major turn-off. Watching her television show for the first time, I was reminded of a mom I once knew who'd amputate your fingers if you tried to sneak a taste of her cookie dough. Martha claimed to enjoy doing homey things for other people, yet she had the personality of a kitchen witch.

Over time, though, I got used to her edginess. I grew to admire her talents, too, especially the way she spun her cozy crafts and catering business into several multi-million dollar industries. Her publishing empire alone, including books, magazines, and a syndicated newspaper column, boasts circulation figures in the millions.

I also became a major fan of her Kmart products, including the stylish Martha Stewart Everyday line. (Just in case she lands in jail, I've already stocked up on her white porcelain serving dishes, kitchen towels, and culinary gadgets.) And I still drink my morning coffee in a Martha mug.

More than anything, though, I credit Martha for lending dignity to the term "home keeping" in an era when many of us were treating our houses like hotels.

Martha made roasting a turkey look easy enough to do in my own kitchen—something I'd never had the courage to try until I watched her television program. She elevated even the most casual meal to an art form, reminding us that there's more to the good life than working our butts off and coming home to eat dinner out of a box or a can. She also showcased the creative talents of other men and women who excelled in the domestic arts. In her own irascible way, she set out to prove that one's home is one's castle, and is always worth the extra effort.

Like her or not, there never will be another Martha Stewart. But last week, homemakers across the country were asking the same question: Can another domestic diva possibly replace her? Martha wannabes are donning their aprons.

Chris Casson Madden, a nationally syndicated columnist and author of several interior design books, will market a new product line at JCPenney this spring. Rachel Ashwell (of Shabby Chic fame) and Tracy Porter already launched their own bed linens and ceramic knick-knacks at Target.

I don't envy any of these women.

I'm beginning to think that laboring in obscurity isn't such a bad thing. As the old adage goes, a name that has become too famous is too heavy a burden to bear. That's especially true in America, where, more often than not, celebrity is just another flash in the frying pan.

We delight in placing the most unlikely people on pedestals—whether they play football or design ceramic teapots. And, oh, how we love to hear them crash when they fall.

———————

Blackout

August 24, 2003

---

lectricity is something we've always taken for granted—until about 4:10 P.M. on August 14th, when the largest blackout in North American history zapped virtually every life line in suburban Detroit.

Refrigerators and air-conditioners stopped humming. Phone lines went dead. Computer screens and TV sets blinked off. The ensuing stillness was sinister and eerie, like a scene from *The Day the Earth Stood Still.* For most of us, it was impossible not to think of September 11, 2001.

A column I was typing vanished in cyberspace, but by the time I learned we'd be fumbling through the whole humid weekend without power, well, missing a newspaper deadline was the least of my worries. Who'd have guessed we'd be boiling tap water or frying eggs on a barbecue in the summer of 2003? Who'd have guessed there'd be a ban on flushing our toilets?

The power outage was, if nothing else, a lesson in humility. And throughout the ordeal, I kept thinking of the quirky folk wisdom my grandmother used to repeat when I was growing up:

Keep the pantry stocked for the unexpected…

Hunger is the best sauce…

Half a loaf is better than none…

Having survived rural life in the windblown Orkney Islands, then the Great Depression after moving to Detroit, Grandma Ruby wouldn't have been fazed by a mere thirty-two-hour blackout. She would have chuckled at the breathless news anchor who dubbed it "a national emergency of epic proportions."

But like most emergencies, this one rekindled primitive survival instincts, and sent us all scurrying to attics or basements in search of rotary phones and transistor radios. Hunting for a lighter, I couldn't help but laugh at the irony. And had I kept one of those gratitude journals recommended by self-help authors, the gas range in our kitchen and the gas grill in the backyard would have topped my list.

Next would follow, in no particular order: bottled spring water; instant coffee; my glow-in-the-dark watch; a manual can opener; the new box of candles I found in a kitchen cupboard; a transistor radio; three flashlights; spare batteries; and a stash of Mrs. Field's chocolate chip cookies.

Thanks to our gas range, which we ignited with a barbecue lighter, my family and I were able to boil water and cook several meals throughout the weekend. Our neighbors with electric ranges weren't so lucky—and most restaurants nearby were closed.

We hadn't stocked up on groceries prior to the blackout, but we did manage to rustle up enough pasta, zucchini, and tomato sauce to feed a small army of local loved ones. It was a simple supper—not something we'd ordinarily serve company—but suddenly that didn't seem to matter. For once, we were strictly aiming for sustenance and making good use of what we had on hand.

Later that weekend, after our power was restored and the leftovers in our refrigerator had melted, I made a beeline to the grocery store with my emergency shopping list. Many of the shelves were depleted; some ravaged. Regardless, I found what I needed, and couldn't recall the last time I'd felt so thrilled to be in a supermarket. Filling my cart with staples, I promised myself that I will never underestimate the power of a manual can opener and a stockpile of canned tomato sauce.

And from now on, I will always keep the pantry stocked for the unexpected.

What's For Dinner?

October 29, 2001

---

*"It is not just the Great Works of mankind that make a culture.
It is the daily things, like what people eat and how they serve it."*
—Laurie Colwin

The November issue of *Gourmet* arrived last week.
The cover features a beautifully roasted turkey perched on a silver platter and encircled with traditional Thanksgiving side dishes. It's an inspiring work of culinary art, yet somehow it stirs in me unbearable waves of incompetence and makes me wonder: Why on earth do we do this every year?

For most Americans, the *Gourmet* photograph represents the ultimate American meal—an emotionally loaded ritual that binds us closer together. It evokes warm-fuzzy images of cheerful grandmothers fussing in the kitchen, nuclear families pulling their Windsor chairs to the table in unison, and fathers leading everyone in prayer.

But that's Norman Rockwell's version, isn't it?

The way most of us eat every day—out of a can or straight from the box—tells another story entirely.

Today, the ordinary family meal seems to be going the way of the drive-in movie. Nutritionists warn that we're becoming a grossly overfed nation of snackers. Always on the run, we munch alone in the car between phone calls, or gobble at the kitchen counter between errands. Even family psychologists warn that we're missing a nourishing part of human civilization when we don't gather at the table to break our daily bread.

Yet every aspect of modern living, from business meetings to soccer practice, makes it impossible for most families to share a pot roast every night at 6:00. Routine trips to the supermarket are weighted with anxiety. Conflicting health fads bombard us at every turn; nearly everything we'd love to eat makes us fat or reputedly makes us ill. And who has time to follow those complicated recipes in a magazine?

"Many home cooks feel compelled to replicate the most complicated dishes before they deem themselves good cooks," explains Michele Urvater, in her *Monday to Friday Cookbook* (Workman).

Urvater, a professional cook and star of a television food series, admits that even she was "frequently too tired or too lazy" to cook for her own family. She also overdosed on carry-out cuisine before designing a variety of family meals that are easy to prepare and clean up. Part of her solution, which seems to help most working parents today, includes "one-pot" recipes that are simple enough for a youngster to follow.

I also like the way she gives us permission to improvise; even to cook eggs and toast for dinner.

"People, women especially, should not feel they are failing their families if they don't manage to cook a three-course dinner every night of the week," Urvater advises. What really counts, she says, is the companionship around the table.

So, whatever works for you—hot dogs or Cordon Bleu—here's a toast to the ordinary family meal.

Creature Comforts

Willie

July 12, 2003

"We've worked hard to exile ourselves from nature, yet we end up longing for what we've lost: a sense of connectedness."
—Diane Ackerman

As long as I've had a garden, I've done battle with squirrels and lost most of the skirmishes. Squirrels have pilfered my prettiest container gardens, ripping out impatiens and petunias and leaving them for dead on the patio. Not stopping there, the furry little pirates also like to bury acorns in my perennial beds and shoplift my daffodil bulbs.

Several years ago, I read in *Country Living* that squirrels have relatively large brains for such small rodents, which explains how they manage to outwit your best attempts to keep them out of the birdfeeder.

So, I was just about ready to strangle them all—until I met Willie.

My family's relationship with Willie began this spring over a jar of honey roasted peanuts. Relaxing on our patio one weekend, Doug absentmindedly tossed a handful of nuts to some squirrels playing in the yard. Sniffing an opportunity, Willie was the smartest in the bunch and began returning daily for the next windfall.

In my initial ignorance of squirrel anatomy, I named Willie after a male hamster I owned as a child. By the time Doug got a closer look at Willie's undercarriage, which proved beyond a doubt that Willie was capable of nursing a litter of baby squirrels, it was too late. To us, Willie was a "he" and we couldn't quite shake the pronoun.

Doug was the first to train Willie to take peanuts from his hand, and soon the whole family was charmed. Word traveled quickly through the neighborhood, too, making Willie a local celebrity. He was even featured in a photo project for Nate's high-school French class.

Genius that he is, Willie also discovered where I write every morning. Leaping onto the Rose of Sharon bush next to my study window, he'll show up routinely at 10:30. Once he makes eye contact through the window, he zips to a nearby garden bench and waits for me to meet him with a jar of nuts. And this little guy knows how to woo me. He'll sit right next to me on the bench while he nibbles, holding his treat with monkey-like fingers and gazing back at me with bright black eyes.

I've asked myself why I find this so entertaining; why I'd bother befriending a nervy little rodent when I have bigger chores on my list. As naturalist Diane Ackerman suggests, I suppose it has something to do with a longing to reconnect with the natural world. Backyard animals like Willie are, in a way, a living link to that world.

Surfing the Web, I found a link to "The Squirrel Almanac," which is maintained by a biologist and contains everything you'd ever want to know about squirrels, and then some. I learned that Willie is a fox squirrel, the largest of the arboreal (tree) squirrels. Since wildlife in the suburbs is fraught with peril, fox squirrels rarely live past seven years. (Who can predict when a random BMW might plow into one of the daredevils crossing the boulevard?)

Which is why I was so upset last week when I spotted a dead fox squirrel near the curb, just a few yards away from the silver maple that Willie calls home. Suddenly, road kill wasn't just a term for anonymous casualties.

But thank heaven for small miracles. Willie returned promptly at 10:30 the next morning for his daily ration of nuts, reminding me once again that it doesn't take much to make my day.

———————

Eulogy for a
Very Fine Cat

November 29, 2001

I didn't fall apart when I found his orange flea collar in my desk drawer. And I was totally in control when I hung his "Cat's First Christmas" ornament on the tree.

It was the picture of the cat on the 5.5 oz. Friskies can that did it—sent me running in tears to the public restroom at the supermarket. The tabby on the can looked a lot like Whiskers, the family pet who'd wrapped his stripped tail around my daily routine for the past six years.

Of all the cats that ever lived with us (and there have been quite a few) Whisk was the hardiest. Or so we'd thought.

A husky marmalade tabby, Whisk naturally assumed the role of alpha cat, even though he'd been neutered as a kitten. He insisted on eating his meals before the other cats in our household, and while this might have seemed greedy, he often expressed his gratitude by leaving dead chipmunks on our porch. As my neighbor told me last year, Whisk earned his coveted reputation as the best "chipmunker" in Oakland County.

He was a showoff.

Despite his prowess, he had a tender side and would sometimes offer nose nudges on cue.

Always a good listener, Whisk took an interest in my writing career, and was never bored by any draft I read aloud in my study. His presence there was as predictable and welcome as my morning mug of coffee. He'd perch complacently on my desk until late afternoon, a furry orange Buddha waiting for the hum of an electric can opener.

So, it was only fitting I discovered, after the veterinarian took an X-ray, that Whisk had a very large heart. A dangerously enlarged heart, in fact, had thrown him into the final stage of cardiac failure by the time we'd reached the steel examination table at the animal emergency clinic. The only humane option was to put him out of his misery.

"Do you want us to cremate him, or will you take him home and bury him yourself?" the veterinarian asked gently after Whisk had gone to meet his maker. It was over that quickly.

One last time, I drove Whisk home in the blue pet carrier he'd learned to dread as a kitten. Then I waited for my husband to come home and help me bury him outside my study windows.

Later that week, the holiday season began. My friend Annie, a fellow cat lover, dropped off a poinsettia and a sympathy card with a poem titled "In the Loss of Your Pet." The verse on the card assured "there must be a heaven for the animal friends we love."

I know some theologians will argue that pets—whether we're talking gerbils or German shepherds—don't go to heaven and are only allowed to sprawl on the furniture in limbo, if anywhere at all. So I appreciated these comforting lines from Annie's card:

Pets bring out our own humanity.
Each day they teach us little lessons in trust
and steadfast affection.
Whatever heaven may be, there's surely a place in it
for friends as good as these.

A reader told me recently that losing her spaniel was harder than losing a member of her human family. "It's been months since Bud was put to sleep," she said, "but the house still seems way too empty without him."

Oh yes, how well I know.

———————

A Fine-feathered Easter

April 11, 2004

W hen you really think about it, Americans do strange things to celebrate religious holidays.

Consider Easter. There's nothing particularly pious about hiding neon pink and blue plastic eggs in the backyard. And it's not exactly Christian to give someone a milk-chocolate rabbit, especially if the recipient is on the Atkins diet.

Even more bewildering was the pair of live ducklings my uncle gave me for Easter when I was a child. I don't recall the looks on my parents' faces when my uncle handed me the cardboard box containing two fuzzy ducklings peeping at the tops of their tiny lungs. But I remember being told right away that I couldn't keep them both.

A neighborhood playmate agreed to adopt one of the ducklings, but after a couple of weeks the poor thing was sent to a relative's farm up north, where it became a holiday dinner entree the following spring. For lack of a better idea, my parents bought a small swimming pool and reluctantly allowed me keep my duckling in our back-yard.

Like most suburbanites, my mom and dad were totally clueless about livestock, so our new pet initially stirred up some gender confusion. As the weeks passed, the duck I had named Oliver matured and sprouted a mass of dazzling white feathers.

Raised in rural Scotland, my grandfather knew immediately that Oliver was really an Olivia.

"A male duck has a curl at the end of his tail," Grandpa insisted. "The females have a plain tail like Oliver's." It wasn't long before Grandpa had additional proof. One morning, Oliver left a large egg in the small shed where she slept—and from then on, we found a fresh egg in her bedding every day.

Of course, it took the neighbors a while to get used to our exceptional pet. Some were startled when they first heard Oliver's daily wake-up quack around 7:00 A.M. And Mrs. Ritchie, who lived on the street behind us, says she still remembers watching the duck waddle next to me whenever I visited my friends around the block.

Oliver was no bird brain. She never let me out of her sight when she was away from home. But as soon as she recognized our house, she'd high-tail it back to her blue plastic swimming pool in the back-yard.

She was also sharp enough to understand it was feeding time whenever she heard the sound of a spoon banging on the side of a dish. Her diet consisted mostly of dried corn from a nearby feed store, or a plate of finely chopped, hard-boiled eggs. For dessert she enjoyed the pansies in my mother's garden.

If her wake-up quack didn't produce the desired result, Oliver would nibble at the screen on my bedroom window in the morning. When I appeared outside, she would bow and stretch her long neck in greeting, which always thrilled me.

In retrospect, Oliver wasn't the easiest pet to care for, and today I wouldn't recommend keeping a duck for a pet in the suburbs. Backyard captivity isn't fair to any creature that ordinarily thrives in a rural setting. (If you're still not convinced, a recent phone call to our local Code Enforcement department confirmed that there's an ordinance against keeping live ducks and chickens on residential property.)

At the end of Oliver's second summer with us, we returned from a family vacation to discover she had died in our backyard. The neighbor who was caring for her could only guess that she'd been attacked by a predatory animal.

Oliver's stay with us was brief but eventful, and it sparked my near-religious devotion to birds and animals. Years later, I can't think of Easter without remembering her.

Booger

August 14, 2002

---

*"Cats seem to go on the principle that it never does
any harm to ask for what you want."*
—Joseph W. Krutch

Sensitive friends reminded us that "Booger" is an awful name
for anything, even a vagrant cat. But when we found him
huddled on our porch on the coldest day in February five
years ago, we assumed he was on a winter vacation, looking for a
warm hotel. Besides, "Booger" sounded like a good nickname for a
black-and-white stray that looked and smelled as if he were part
skunk.

Since we already owned three cats and hadn't planned to adopt
another, the family launched an all-out campaign to help Booger
locate his rightful owner. Nate, who was twelve at the time, made
FOUND CAT posters on our computer and distributed them all over
town. I purchased classified ad space in the local paper. But for all
that effort, we didn't uncover a single lead. One neighbor guessed

that Booger's owners dumped him off on our boulevard because they were moving to a new home or tired of buying cat food. Over the years our neighborhood had become the unofficial county depot for unwanted, pre-owned pets.

Meanwhile, "Boog" maneuvered his way from the porch into our living room. And it didn't take him long to develop a preference for 9 Lives Super Supper and the softest cushions in the house. Still, he remained somewhat aloof, orphan that he was, and flatly refused to be confined indoors.

What surprised me was how quickly I took to *him*. Something in the way he sprawled on his back conveyed sincere gratitude. And once I'd earned his trust, he let on that he liked having his belly scratched. Hard as I tried, though, I couldn't reform his hobo habits.

The day after Halloween that year, Boog dragged himself inside our back door, unable to put any weight on his rear legs. Attempting to crawl upstairs to his hiding place in my closet, he collapsed on the third step and moaned.

That evening, Doug and I drove him to a twenty-four-hour emergency clinic, where a veterinarian ordered an x-ray. Boog, the doctor suspected, was the victim of a "blunt trauma." We could only guess what that meant: A Halloween prankster might have kicked him or thrown something on his spine, leaving his back legs and tail partially paralyzed. In any event, the prognosis wasn't hopeful. If Boog didn't regain use of his legs in a month, the alternative would be expensive surgery or, more likely, euthanasia.

"You might want to put him out of his misery now, rather than later," the vet advised.

By then it was midnight, and we were totally exhausted, so we paid the $135 bill and rode home with Boog wrapped in my terrycloth bathrobe.

Over the next three weeks, Boog dutifully swallowed his prescribed cortisone tablets. And in a solicitous gesture, which my family deemed purely ridiculous, I arranged his bedding on an electric heating pad, hoping the warmth would somehow heal his injuries.

All of that is history now, and I'm thrilled to report that Boog finally regained the use of his legs and tail. He's still an alley cat at heart, yet he always limps back to our house, where he gobbles two huge meals a day and sleeps in my bathroom sink. I think he's planning to stay.

The cat has no style, no dignity, and only a few lives left. But he's taught me a thing or two about hanging on when the odds are stacked against you, and I've grown to admire his sheer audacity.

Work Ethics

Go Ahead,
Make My Day

September 5, 2004

Placing my order in the drive-thru line of a fast-food restaurant, I was pleasantly surprised by the woman who responded on the speaker. Upbeat and professional, her Diane Sawyer-like delivery changed my perception of the restaurant—so much so, in fact, that I mentioned it when I pulled up to the window for my onion rings.

"Wow, thanks for the compliment!" she answered, obviously as stunned as she was pleased. "Nobody's ever said that before."

I shared this little episode with an editor who agreed that few of us are used to hearing praise or applause these days. (Journalists, after all, endure more public scolding on a daily basis than any other profession.)

And you don't have to read the viewpoint pages to realize there are an awful lot of folks out there who've managed to turn griping and nitpicking into a full-time hobby. Maybe it's human nature to derive pleasure from pointing out everything that's wrong in the world, from errors of grammar to fashion mistakes. Or maybe it's symptomatic of a clinically crabby culture. Either way, lately I've noticed that people would just as soon flip you the bird from behind a car window as say something nice to you in person. How sad is that?

I don't mean to imply that we shouldn't be held accountable for our mistakes. Criticism often paves the road to improvement. But if negative criticism is all we hear, well, it's just plain demoralizing.

That's why I've made it my mission to practice a new approach: I catch others doing something right, and then I tell them so. It really isn't as radical as it sounds, especially if you keep in mind that paying a compliment needn't be such a big deal. Praise shouldn't be confused with flattery, nor should it be saved for special occasions like award banquets, retirement parties, and funerals.

If the dinner special is outstanding, for example, I simply ask the waiter to share my review with the chef. If my new haircut is especially flattering, I'm just as generous with my kudos as I am with my stylist's tip. If my son takes extra care with his household chores, I tell him that his effort didn't go unnoticed. And if a girlfriend shows up in a sharp new outfit, I tell her how terrific she looks.

As corny as it sounds, I really do feel better when I make others feel good. Even Mark Twain, our greatest American cynic, once admitted that he could "live for two months on a good compliment."

I also believe that every piece of mean-spirited criticism we hurl, whether it's a spiteful comment about a coworker's promotion or a lethal letter to the editor, will eventually fly back in our faces like a pie in a Three Stooges film.

An impressive body of medical research indicates that chronic complainers are more likely to suffer from chronic diseases, including cancer. Negativity is highly contagious, which is why nobody likes to hang around people who make a habit of it.

This summer, I finished two books by an author whose elegant prose lifted me higher and made me feel like a better person for having read his work. At the end of each book, he extended this invitation: "I always enjoy hearing from readers and fellow pilgrims, and sincerely hope you'll write and tell me what you think."

Someday, when I've finished grumbling about my lack of free time, I'm going to sit down and write that guy a nice letter.

The Family Paper Trail

June 21, 2003

Newspaper careers tend to run in families.

My great-great grandfather was a foreign correspondent based in Washington D.C., and while my work isn't nearly as glamorous, I must have inherited his passion for newsprint. And I shouldn't have been surprised this year when Nate decided to run for the editorship of his high-school newspaper—and won.

I've always been careful not to push Nate in the direction of my own career, such as it is, but I discovered several years ago that printer's ink runs in his blood, too. As soon as he turned twelve, the kid begged for his own paper route.

His dad and I were ambivalent, at first, and secretly relieved to learn that no routes for the local daily were available. But following a major blizzard that winter, Nate got a call with the good news: A route had opened up in our neighborhood. He couldn't wait to get started.

"I hope you know what you're getting into," another parent

warned me. "Not only are you writing for the paper, Cindy, but you'll be delivering it, too."

Soon after, mammoth stacks of papers arrived daily on our porch. Rubber bands, plastic bags, fliers, and other delivery doodads littered every surface in the house. But in retrospect, I think it was worth the hassle.

The smart-alecky seventh-grader got a sharp taste of the business world. He learned that customers expected his product on time, regardless of whether he was late from school or had "tons of math homework." He discovered that readers were paying for the convenience of home delivery, not for papers tossed in puddles on the sidewalk. He learned the diplomacy required of every bill collector, as well as how to balance accounts when money was due. This was real-life math.

He also found that the biggest challenge for any newspaper carrier is crawling out of bed before sunrise on Sunday mornings—hours before the local pastors have opened their Bibles. Though Nate covered his own route on weekdays, his dad and I helped deliver the bulkier Sunday papers at dawn. Other parents told us we were spoiling the kid by chauffeuring him block to block when we could have been sleeping in, but I never saw it that way.

There was magic in those Sunday mornings. Since I've never been an early riser, it was a rare gift to watch the sun rise. In the summer, especially, the color show was spectacular—neon streaks of lavender, orange, and gold flashing above the treetops on the suburban skyline.

As each bundled newspaper hit its targeted porch, it also struck me that my relationship with this gangly boy had morphed overnight into a tug-of-war between my moody middle age and his stubborn adolescence. His boyhood was ending too quickly.

"Please... slow... down!" I'd holler as he frantically scaled porch steps, two by two, trying to finish the route before 9:00 A.M.

The cheerful camaraderie we'd shared in the early grade-school years had recently given way to recurring battles over household messes and Internet use, but during the time we worked the neighborhood route we were back on common ground. If only for an hour or so a week, we were a team again.

To everyone's surprise, Nate kept that job for nearly two years, quitting it only because homework and high-school commitments had to take priority.

It was a learning experience for the whole family. We never rushed home after the last paper was delivered, but made a special ritual of stopping for hot chocolate and hash browns. The rest of the day, and its deadlines, could wait.

———————————

Service with a Shrug?

December 9, 1998

"No race can prosper till it learns there is as much dignity
in tilling a field as in writing a poem."
—Booker T. Washington

It's the advent of the holiday shopping season, and commercialism is as rampant as canned music renditions of "Jingle Bells." Which is why I hesitate to admit that one of my favorite places to buy holiday lights is a hardware store that's part of a vast national chain—a chain that doesn't need a plug from a local journalist.

Still, when any business, large or small, delivers a fine product and tops it off with congenial service, well, it's something to write home about.

The routine at the hardware is pretty simple. I wander the aisles; an employee notices my bewilderment and asks if I need assistance. I'm escorted to the proper shelf, and then left in peace to ponder my decision.

But it's the guy working the check-out counter on the evening shift who always makes my night. Looking me in the eye, he asks, "Hey, how's it goin'? How's your evening?" as if my answer will mean something to him. When I respond with, "Fine, thanks, how about yours?" he tells me he couldn't be better, that life is terrific.

It's an ordinary exchange of pleasantries, I know, yet the man behaves as if there's nothing he'd rather be doing at the moment than bagging my picture hooks and light bulbs. Unfortunately, this scenario is an exception, not the rule. When was the last time you patronized a business and left feeling delighted with the service as well as the product? How many times have you been greeted with a smile and an upbeat attitude? Or are you typically ignored while standing at a counter, waiting for a salesperson to wander over or at least acknowledge your presence?

If you think the service you're getting is generally worse than it used to be, you're not alone. According to Matthew Gilbert, author of *Take This Job and Love It* (Daybreak Books), a 1997 Gallup poll revealed that while fifty-three percent of all respondents gave high marks to the quality of U.S. products, a mere thirty-six percent gave similar ratings to the quality of service.

"Thirty-one percent felt the quality of service they receive has been in decline, with employee attitude topping the list of reasons," Gilbert noted. And consider this: The U.S. Bureau of Labor has predicted that by the year 2005, "service-producing jobs will account for the majority of all future job growth," with service workers expected to add 4.6 million jobs.

In other words, we could be doomed to shuffle through another century of crabby cashiers, cranky fast-food workers, bored waiters, and depleted day-care providers.

Part of the problem, Gilbert suggests, is that American service workers "continue to be stigmatized as poor and undereducated, thus demeaning their contribution to the economic, social, and spiritual fabric." Most service jobs are viewed as means to an end, rarely as honorable careers.

If we keep measuring our worth on the competitive scale of material success—affluent income, prestigious degrees, expensive cars and clothing—we'll continue to belittle work that doesn't earn these rewards. And it follows that if we treat or regard service workers as inferior humans, we shouldn't be so surprised to get less than what we're paying for.

Yet there is dignity in all work, and all work can have spiritual as well as material value, Gilbert believes.

Work, he says, is terribly undervalued as a source of inspiration. "This is no less true for the street sweeper and the shoeshine man than it is for those in any other profession."

But inspiration doesn't come easily, especially to the workers whose job description includes daily confrontations with hamburger grease, abrasive customers, and screaming kids. They could use a generous helping of our compassion.

The road to cordial relations never was a one-way street. An overall shift in attitude could vastly improve the quality of the basic products and services that support our economy, our way of life.

———————

The Slings and Arrows of Rejection

November 2, 1997

"Every rejection slip was like the rejection of me, myself."
—Madeleine L'Engle

I meet them every time I attend a cocktail party or a business function.

They're the stressed-out professionals who'd love to quit their jobs and try "something more fun." Most of them want to get published. I was cornered by one of these aspiring authors at a seminar last month. A colleague of my husband's, the man works as a designer for a high-profile architecture firm, but he really wants to be recognized for his byline.

The colleague said he wrote essays occasionally. He had experienced the fleeting thrill of seeing a couple of his pieces in the local paper—"a real high," as he put it. He wanted to publish more often in Sunday newspaper magazines, and he wanted to earn some money for his writing. After receiving several rejection letters, however, he was ready to give up.

"How do you handle the rejection? I hate rejection," he said.

"The same way architects do when their building designs are rejected," I told him.

"Oh, no," he shot back. "That's not as personal."

Rejection and its evil twin, Criticism, are part and parcel of the writing life. I don't care much for either of them, yet both keep in touch with me periodically. And while it's true that rejection letters can sting for a few days, eventually you get used to them. You learn to accept the fact that you can't hit the editorial bull's-eye every time.

A fellow writer once offered this consolation, and I believe she's right: If you're not getting rejection slips, you're not aiming high enough or sending out enough material. You have to toughen up, get busy, and hold your breath every time you open the mailbox. More often than not, you start the process all over again.

As I reminded the guy from the architecture firm, "personal" rejection is hardly the sole province of publishing. *Anything* you dearly hope to achieve, including love itself, holds the possibility of loss. That said, I agree that the very word "rejection" dissolves bone marrow and turns warm blood to ice water. On a really bad day, it can make even the most aggressive self-promoter drop her best ideas and run home.

That's why I often share a favorite story about Madeleine L'Engle, whose award-winning children's book, *A Wrinkle in Time,* was rejected by more than forty publishers before it finally went to press. L'Engle believed in her book, believed in its power to inspire children, and absolutely refused to let it die. Today it remains a beloved best-seller for young people.

It also helps to remember that the craft of writing offers second and third chances. As Frank Lloyd Wright said, "A doctor can bury his mistakes, but an architect can only advise his client to plant vines." Thankfully, redemption is so much easier for writers. We can reorganize, revise, revamp, and send our stuff out into the world again.

But the real secret to coping with rejection—aside from keeping faith in your own abilities—is to enjoy the process, the work itself. You have to fall in love with words and take pleasure in the way you string them together. And it's essential to remember that publishing, as novelist Anne Lamott once said, is an addictive drug. Your last conquest will never feel like enough.

Still, the small victories are sweet. Not long ago, one of my favorite pieces was rejected by a regional magazine. Several postage stamps later, it was accepted by a national publication for more money than I'd expected—and I hadn't changed a word.

That doesn't happen as often as I'd like, of course. Just often enough to fuel my hopes and make my work more fun than architecture.

Domestic Diva Comes Clean

December 3, 2000

he first chilly day of the season is enough to send most people outdoors to prepare the garden for winter, or to the hardware store to stock up on snow shovels and rock salt. Not me. I throw myself into domestic overdrive—inside the house.

Down from the top bookshelves come my soup-and-bread cookbooks. Out of storage comes the slow cooker. And off to the grocery I go to stock up on peas, beans, cornmeal, barley, and other staples that rarely take up pantry space in the summer.

Making soup from scratch is one of my favorite autumn rituals. By four o'clock, my writing deadlines have been met, and it's time to sauté vegetables in the kitchen while Oprah chats up her guests. Like cookbook author Molly O'Neil, I find "reassurance in the aroma of baking bread and simmering stews." Life doesn't get much cozier than this.

Until recently, though, I was always a little embarrassed to flaunt my domestic side. That was before I was introduced to the work of Cheryl Mendelson, who describes herself as a working woman with "a secret life."

She adores keeping house.

Mendelson is a lawyer, professor, and author of *Home Comforts: The Art & Science of Keeping House* (Scribner). Weighing in at 884 pages, her hefty guide is the first of its kind to be published by one author in nearly a century. It contains everything you need to know (and some things you don't) about stocking a pantry, setting a proper table, hemming a skirt, building a fire, and deodorizing pet stains.

"By the time I reached young adulthood," she explains in her introduction, "modern suburbia had little interest in housekeeping and even less respect for it." Like many women of my generation, Mendelson threw herself into a career and spent a few years posturing as "anti-domestic."

After work, while poring over her collection of vintage housekeeping manuals, Mendelson began to suspect that men and women of the post-Betty Crocker era could use some basic home economics training. It didn't take much research to prove her theory.

"Over and over I found myself visiting homes where the predominant feeling was sepulchral, dusty, and deserted, or even hotel-like, as my own had once become," she recalls. "It's housekeeping that makes your home alive and turns it into a small society in its own right."

Mendelson's standards are a lot higher than mine. She lists, for example, more than a dozen "common" food pathogens that were never covered in my biology classes. She also insists that the "most effective" floor-washing is done on hands and knees. Not in my house. But she's right on target when she claims that the domestic arts deserve a lot more attention and a little respect.

Apparently many homemakers agree, since sales figures for her book remain healthy. This bodes well for other domestic divas who've labored in secret for years. And just imagine: If a Harvard law school grad can revel in housework and publish a best-selling book about it, well, maybe the rest of us can finally come out of the broom closet.

Hooked on the Net

January 18, 1998

"Most of us are about as eager to be changed as we were to be born, and go through our changes in a similar state of shock."
                                        —James Baldwin

If you'd told me last year that I would be using the Internet every day, I wouldn't have believed you. I came late to the computer, or maybe I should say the computer came late to me. I was already thirty-four when I learned how to use a word processor, and only reluctantly admitted it was the best invention since my electric typewriter. Even after I bought my first PC, it took me months to discover it had a spell-checking option.

Unlike the average ten-year-old, I was terrified of new technology. Initially refusing to set foot on the information highway, I was sure the Internet was a threat to community life as we know it, and would turn us all into a soulless nation of robots and recluses.

But I lightened up a bit when one of my newspaper editors offered to teach me how to use my modem, the part on a computer that would enable me to send my columns over the phone lines. Sending that first article seemed like launching a rocket to Pluto, and I know the editor got tired of hearing, "Now, *which button* do I push?" But when it finally worked, I felt as if I had participated in some sort of miracle. I like to write in my bathrobe, and the modem made it possible to get published without ever leaving the house.

That was only the beginning.

Last year, Nate finally talked me into getting an e-mail address. One major glitch: We couldn't connect my "prehistoric PC" (his description) to the Internet, so my messages had to be routed through the family computer. For a few days, Nate dutifully checked my e-mail and printed any messages I'd received. But he quickly tired of this routine and insisted that I increase his allowance, or else find my own way through cyberspace.

"It's time to learn, Mom," he said. "And time to upgrade your equipment."

The child was right. The Internet could make my research easier. My national editors were already starting to ask if I could e-mail my articles, and I was deeply ashamed to admit I wasn't connected. In other words, the Internet wasn't just a convenient option. My career depended on it.

And so it was that I found myself loading strange software on my brand-new computer after the holiday clearance sales. Like a kid with a toy, I played nonstop. One night I stayed up until 3:00 A.M., sending messages to anyone I could locate with an e-mail address, including Oprah.

Even Nate started getting worried.

"I can't believe you changed your mind about the Internet," he said, eyeing me suspiciously. I think he wanted his old mom back— the mom who cooked dinner on time and complained when *he* spent too much time on the computer.

Now I understand why this brave new technology is so addictive. An entire universe of possibilities glimmers at my fingertips—

local and international news, medical advice, genealogical research, new recipes, book reviews, weather reports, clothing catalogs, and more.

Of course, e-mail can't replace the old-fashioned civility of a handwritten letter or the thrill of a long-distance phone call from an old friend. But I have to admit it's an easy and economical way to stay in touch and to order new shoes.

Best of all, I'm totally convinced that the Internet will reinforce, even expand, our global network—although I still haven't heard back from Oprah.

Puttering

September 6, 2003

A utumn doesn't officially begin until September 23, but for most of us, Labor Day is summer's grand finale. Maybe you're good and ready for cider mills, football season, and fisherman sweaters. But if you've just closed your cottage up north or returned from a dreamy tour of Europe, getting back to routine can feel like a letdown.

You'll need a permission slip for an afternoon of guilt-free puttering.

Cheaper than air fare or psychotherapy, puttering lets your mind wander while your body hangs out around the house. And unlike fall housecleaning, which involves physical energy and high-powered appliances, puttering puts you in a Zen-like state of bliss. Not to be confused with slacking, fidgeting, fiddling, or piddling, puttering is good for mental health.

Sadly, ours is a goal-directed, work-till-you-drop culture. And since most of us like to boast about how terribly busy we are, puttering is never easy to pull off.

For those who practice on the sly, like I do, puttering styles are varied and highly personal. Puttering can be the act of sorting through a box of college textbooks in the basement; tinkering under the hood of an old Chevy; or rearranging things on a shelf while you listen to jazz on the stereo. In other words, puttering is a way of clarifying life's myriad details, especially when it's done with reverence for the objects at hand. It's an opportunity to reconsider what we most enjoy in our homes, and to make a mental list of what we'd like to edit later.

Feeling sluggish and blue last week, I decided to putter in the kitchen. Taking inventory of my good china, I lost myself in happy memories of the two grandmothers who had actually used all the serving pieces for holiday dinners. I marveled, too, at how both sets of dishes have survived several moves and kitchen renovations—and somehow outlived their original owners.

If puttering still sounds like a chore you've postponed, it's only because you haven't found a method that cheers or relaxes you. One man's notion of drudgery, after all, can be another's idea of soul craft.

"I can't explain it, but I enjoy doing dishes," writes Thomas Moore, a former Catholic monk and author of the best-selling *Care of the Soul*. "I've had an automatic dishwasher in my home for over a year, and I have never used it. What appeals to me, I think, is the reverie induced by going through the ritual of washing, rinsing, and drying." Thomas Moore can come over to my house and wash dishes any time he visits Detroit (especially if his visit coincides with another power failure). Meanwhile, I'll keep loading my dishwasher.

Still, there's merit in savoring the ordinary tasks of daily living.

A lot of us spend our lives reaching for lofty goals, or at least trying to look productive 24/7. This wouldn't be such a bad thing if so many of us weren't scratching our heads and wondering what's missing even after we've won all the trophies. (Consider all those baby-boomer executives who can't wait to retire.)

"My life has no purpose, no direction, no aim, no meaning, and yet I'm happy. I can't figure it out. What am I doing right?" observed Charles M. Schulz, creator of *Peanuts*.

Charlie Brown, after all, was pretty good at puttering.

––––––––––––––

Family Album

A Photo of My Dad

June 12, 2002

It's my favorite photograph of Dad and me—one of those price-less family icons I'd rescue if the house caught fire.

Taken on Father's Day in 1992, it reveals the totally uncompli-cated relationship we'd enjoyed right up to the moment the shutter clicked. I use the word uncomplicated because I can't think of a more lyrical way to describe my father or the way he lived. Even when pop psychologists urged us to scrutinize our parents and find them suspect, I saw my dad as a patient man whose agenda was rarely hidden. He was the kind of guy who appreciated most people just as they were, and I think that's what we all loved best about him.

But let me explain the photograph.

Dad and I were standing on my back porch, having just finished the surprise dinner I'd hosted for him and my father-in-law.

Dad wore a pale blue windbreaker and an outdated pair of glasses that somehow looked right on him. My hair was orange, thanks to a failed experiment with a drugstore highlighting kit. The late afternoon sun shimmered through the maples in our yard, and my mother was anxious to finish the film left in her camera.

Dad and I hugged tightly for the shot.

He was sixty-five and grinning—despite the grim diagnosis of degenerative heart disease he'd been given a few months earlier. At thirty-seven, I was newly unemployed and unsure of my career path. The travel magazine I edited for nearly six years had folded abruptly, dropping me off at midlife without a new map. Still, summer had arrived and we were optimistic. Dad's diabetes was under control, or as he put it, he'd been "feeling pretty darned good lately."

Better yet, the ball games were in full swing. It wasn't shaping up to be a stellar season for the Tigers, but Cecil Fielder and Lou Whitaker were giving it their best. (While I never shared my dad's religious devotion to baseball, I still can't hear the crack of a bat against a ball without remembering the old transistor radio he kept tuned to his games.)

But there's something else about the photo.

Looking at it today, you'd never imagine the two of us had a major-league concern beyond what we'd be eating for dessert that evening. Nor would you guess that this 35mm print chronicled one of our last days together.

The inevitable phone call came two weeks later on a Monday morning: "Your dad collapsed in the driveway. The ambulance is coming."

So this week I'm very grateful for that luminous Father's Day afternoon ten years ago—grateful I hadn't waited another day to throw my dad a surprise party. I usually postpone my good intentions, adding them to a long list of things I plan to do later. Later, when there's more time…

"Today is the only time we can possibly live," wrote Dale Carnegie, whose work my father read often and admired. I see now that Carnegie's philosophy is gleefully captured in my father's grin, which my mother wisely captured on film.

———————

Portrait of an
Artist as Mother

Mother's Day, 1995

L ike most children who grew up in the 1950s, I took for granted
that my mother would be waiting at home each afternoon
when I returned from school. Back then, day-care providers
were called baby-sitters, and typically their employment was limited to occasional Saturday evenings.

The "average housewife" role, now a remnant of that mythical
past, was as indigenous to middle-class suburbia as *The Donna Reed
Show.* Combining what she called "the best of both worlds," my
mother earned a respectable paycheck while working at home, un-
knowingly paving the way for the free-lance writing career I began
after my son was born.

Trained as a commercial artist, Mom applied transparent oil tints
to photographic portraits of brides and high-school graduates. (This
was long before portraiture was changed by the introduction of di-
rect-color film, which is utilized for most photography today.) I remember coming home from school to find Mom working in her por-
table "studio," which was a table pulled next to a window overlook-
ing our backyard. Perched next to her in a small chair, I watched as
she squeezed oil paints onto a glass palette and applied delicate
washes of color to each sepia-toned portrait.

I chattered while she painted, occasionally cleaning her brushes in spirits of turpentine. With an ear tilted toward our conversation, Mom would follow my rambling grade-school chitchat—a daily litany of kids who had misbehaved on the playground, or the impossible words I'd misspelled on a test. During these intimate girl talks, problems were solved, opinions formed, hurts consoled.

I was always proud of her—proud to say, "My mom is an artist."

But until I started my own family, I never fully realized how many times she struggled to meet her deadlines and keep a home. Around the clock she painted her portraits and delivered them in bright yellow Kodak boxes to local photography studios, made meals for my father and me, decorated our home, volunteered at my school, and even found time to help lead a Girl Scout troop.

In my naïve childhood view, at least, she had created the illusion that her time stretched infinitely and that she was always accessible. And so, like a good portrait, my relationship with her was never rushed, but rendered lovingly over time, layer upon layer.

Watching my mother, I've learned that the art of living well has a lot to do with improvisation. You must continually find new ways to use the materials and circumstances at hand.

Shortly after my father's sudden death, Mom had to sell our family home and move to a smaller place. Adjusting to her new identity as a widow was difficult, and I know she missed the home she and my dad had built together. Everyone we knew grieved the abrupt change in our small family.

But surprisingly, even to me, Mom began transforming the new, blank walls of her condominium into a welcoming place of warmth and beauty. Once again, I saw the artist filling her rooms with silk flowers, family antiques, and photographs of favorite people. She reinvented a home for herself.

Art critic John Ruskin once wrote, "When love and skill work together, expect a masterpiece." Reading this maxim, I always think of my mother.

The Family Piano

June 15, 1999

Happy memories don't weigh much and are fairly easy to store, but I'm sorry to say the same isn't true of old pianos. "Do you want to move the piano back to your place?" my Uncle Bob asked recently. "If not, I'll give it away. Nobody's touched it in years."

The piano in question has logged a lot of mileage around southeast Michigan. A handsome mahogany spinet, it first anchored the bay window in the living room of my grandparents' colonial home in northwest Detroit.

It was purchased for my uncle, who took lessons on it when he was a child in the late 1940s. As the story goes, his musical career ended abruptly when he was onstage for his first piano recital. Turning to his parents in the audience, he announced, "I can't do this. I wish I was dead."

After my grandparents died, Uncle Bob's piano ended up at my parents' home, and eventually found its way over to mine after I married. Later on, my uncle moved it to his own home, to "brush up on Chopsticks," as he put it. He also hoped his new grandkids would show an interest in learning Chopin's nocturnes, but that hasn't happened and the poor piano stands neglected in Uncle Bob's living room, waiting for its next sonata.

To me, the instrument is so saturated with memories, right down to the last octave, that donating it to a stranger would strike a melancholy chord in my conscience.

I still remember it in its heyday at my grandparents' home, where it was often played by my great-aunt Annie. She was, as my uncle describes her, a sturdy old maid, having lost her one true love in a car accident. Tireless in her sixties, Annie would arrive daily to help her sister, my Grandma Ruby, whose own health was compromised by a heart condition. Trained to play a mean Scottish fiddle, Annie had great sense of humor and a musical soul.

There wasn't much for a kid to do at my grandparents' home, although I always enjoyed the extra attention I received during visits there. When things got too dull, Annie jazzed them up with her thunderous piano rendition of "Auld Lang Syne," always playing by ear on the black keys. Years of smoking had nearly ruined her voice, but it never kept Annie from belting out old-country folk tunes.

My grandmother, perched on her sofa nearby, smiled indulgently during our Saturday evening recitals. When Annie finished, Grandma Ruby would ask me to play "Danny Boy," one of the first songs I'd learned to play for her. The lyrics were Irish and, to most Scots, terminally corny, but we all loved "Danny Boy" just the same. My grandfather always applauded loudly, proclaiming I was good enough to be on the "Lawrence Welk Show." Then he'd turn the television back on, signaling the concert's finale.

That's why I almost said yes when my uncle asked if I wanted to keep the piano in my house again. I suppose I could have tried to push some furniture around my own living room—a table here, a bookshelf there—to accommodate this bully of a family icon. But we already own another piano that looks better with our things, and we're getting to the age where we need to pare down our possessions, not accumulate more.

After making several phone calls this week, I'm hoping the piano will find its way into someone else's living room, and give voice to another family's favorite tunes.

———————

Grandpa's Ferns

July 5, 1994

My grandfather was the proverbial Scottish curmudgeon, born and bred on a farm in the Orkney Islands. In his last years, his hearty soul hardened a little more; he often barked at the postman and guzzled whiskey from a bottle he insisted on hiding behind the dining room curtains.

But Grandpa had a soft spot or two. One was for me, and the other was for his garden, a veritable jungle of ferns, which, with a battalion of lilies-of-the-valley, hugged the side of his garage.

No other gardener in his west Detroit neighborhood could lay claim to such a crop. Green, tall, and primordial, the ferns had been growing in his backyard for decades. Too modest to call himself a gardener, my grandfather thought of himself simply as caretaker of his ferns. Like Grandpa, the plants were survivors. I'll always associate ferns or "fairrrns," as he pronounced them, with that durable old Scot and the restorative process of grief we experienced together.

I was nine years old when his wife, my favorite grandmother, "passed on," as Grandpa reluctantly explained to those who called for her on the phone. Her death broke our hearts that July, during one of the most humid summers I remember.

Grandpa couldn't put his sorrow into words. He'd spend hours in his easy chair, staring out at the living room in stony silence, listening for the echoes of a voice he'd never hear again. But, young as I was, I knew the moment he began to retrieve his old spirit: I heard him thump out of his recliner, then hobble out to the screened-in porch and into the yard, where his neglected ferns waited.

The whoosh of the garden hose pierced the heavy stillness of the evening. And there my grandfather stood, as he had stood every summer since he had retired, watering his mighty kingdom of ferns. Slipping through the screen door, I ran barefooted across the lawn and joined him.

I inhaled the scent of the fern bouquet, a fragrance like moss in the woods after a warm rain. "That's what the word 'green' would smell like, if it had a smell," I told Grandpa. He nodded in understanding, then retreated to another memory.

For what seemed like hours, Grandpa and I stood in silence, arm in arm, taking turns with the hose and watching the ferns bow and sway under the water's spray. I know we both were thinking of my grandmother and how much we missed her, though neither of us could speak her name aloud. It was then I discovered the secret known to all gardeners: Nature has the mysterious power to console us when words cannot.

Not long before my grandfather sold his house and moved into an apartment, my mother had the foresight to ask him for a few of his ferns. Treasuring them like heirloom silver, my parents and I planted and nurtured the ferns, and carefully took a few with us every time we moved. Over the years we watched them unfurl between rocks and next to porch steps. And we gave them to friends who appreciated them.

Ever since I married and left my parents' home more than twelve years ago, my own little family and I have owned three houses. At each one, I've left behind the green legacy of my grandfather's ferns.

If it's possible to inherit an affinity for gardening and an appreciation of the natural world, then these were my gifts from Grandpa. I never mastered his business skills, and if he were alive today, I doubt he'd understand my poetry. But I think he would approve of the hours I spend with my hands in the soil, sorting out my life's complications with pruning shears and a hand trowel.

Each summer, as the ferns in my yard multiply and flourish, I often slip away to my garden to spend an evening deep in quiet ritual. Waving my garden hose over the delicate fronds, I marvel at how well they have endured so much change and the passing of so many years.

And I always think of Grandpa.

Marian

September 3, 1995

The woman on the phone sounds very nervous. Her name is Susan and she says she's going back to work full-time this month. Susan is looking for a mature woman to care for her five-month-old daughter at home. She wants someone who is dependable and nurturing, a cross between Mary Poppins and Mother Teresa.

Susan is calling because my name is listed as a reference for Marian, the woman who watched Nate in our home years ago when I worked for a travel magazine.

"Were you...happy with Marian?" Susan begins. I know what she's really thinking: *What kind of person is Marian? Can Marian be trusted with my baby?*

Susan can't see that I'm grinning at the other end of the line. I always smile whenever I think of Marian because I'm immediately reminded of Lucille Ball and Fred Rogers. Marian's hair is as red as

Lucy's, and she has the husky voice and giddy sense to humor to match. Not your garden-variety grandmother, Marian teaches Hawaiian dancing and writes poetry in her spare time. Sometimes she wears cowboy boots. And while she's not exactly a fan of Fred Rogers (who's "a little too dull" for her taste) she'll sit patiently through countless reruns of "Mister Rogers' Neighborhood" with any kid who wants to watch them.

"Marian's really great with kids. She's a good sport and has a terrific sense of humor," is the only way I can begin to explain her to Susan.

Like most working mothers I've met, I'm squeamish about day care. Choosing a sitter is an agonizing process, rarely logical. Sometimes you have to go with your gut feeling.

Marian was one of fifteen women who answered my classified ad seeking "Responsible Day Care." But hers was the only voice that sounded just right; she was the only candidate I would interview. Meeting her for the first time in my kitchen, I knew I could trust my instincts.

Marian watched Nate part-time for almost five years, starting when he was fourteen months old. My office hours were flexible at first, usually allowing me to work at home several days each week. But they increased as the magazine grew and my editorial duties expanded. Always a godsend, Marian was able to work around my unpredictable schedule. Meanwhile, when Nate napped, she made our beds or tidied the house—always above and beyond her original job description. One day, for example, she spent her free time reorganizing all the tools in our chaotic garage because she "needed to keep busy."

Nate called Marian "Aunt May-en" until he learned to pronounce the letter R. I remember gut-wrenching moments when he seemed to prefer her company to mine, but I could see why he loved her. Marian had time. While I edited magazine copy, the two of them memorized all the silly lyrics on "Sesame Street," sculpted Play-

Doh animals, drew pictures of Thomas the Tank Engine, and read Dr. Seuss.

Marian had become a family fixture by the time she had to leave us to care for her elderly mother. Shortly thereafter, my magazine folded and I began working full-time at home. After her mother died, Marian resumed her child-care career. Now pushing seventy, she still hasn't run out of energy or enthusiasm. She still calls to stay in touch and to tell us about the new little ones she's babysitting. Sometimes she chats with Nate, who still hasn't forgotten his preschool years with her.

In a card shop last year, I picked up a funny greeting card with a photo of Fred Rogers in his trademark cardigan sweater. I signed it, "We're thinking of you," and mailed it to Marian. As soon as it arrived, she phoned, laughing.

"Can you believe that old fart?" she asked. "He's still on TV and we still have to watch him every day!"

Oh yes, I tell Susan, I'd hire Marian in a heartbeat.

My Wild Irish Relative

March 12, 2000

S o what if historians speculate that St. Patrick was actually born in Roman Britain, possibly near what is known today as Dumbarton, Scotland? He remains the soul of patriotism for the Irish—and those who like to imagine they're Irish—especially this Friday when green beer begins to flow.

To honor St. Pat's Day, many of us will pause to commemorate our own Irish roots, or perhaps to reinvent a distant O'Hara whose vague memory we can toast at a local Celtic pub. Lucky me: I have Russell Irinus Plinius Prime Finney.

Born in 1867, Finney was my maternal great-grandfather, reputedly as quirky and difficult as his full name.

Nobody knows when our branch of the Finneys left Ireland, but according to my mother, Russell Finney's father was a Washington D.C. newspaper correspondent who traveled around the world seven times. Finney's mother, so the story goes, was a real social climber. But young Russell Finney had aspirations of his own. Moving to

Indianapolis at the turn of the century, he married young and followed his bohemian dream of making a living as an artist.

"Just as they do now, most artists struggled to earn an income," my mother recalls. "But Grandpa Finney worked so many hours at his easel that he'd fall asleep on top of a desk in his cluttered studio. For all that, he still lost his commercial clients during the Depression. So he began painting watercolor landscapes to help support his wife and daughter, who quickly lost patience with him."

Always a nature lover, Finney savored his evening walks along the riverbank, sometimes stopping to sketch scenes for his paintings; more often to escape the critical eyes of the women in his life. "His nature walks also worked as excuses to smoke his forbidden cigarettes, since they weren't allowed in the house," my mother adds.

Widowed before World War II, Grandpa Finney packed up his brushes and moved in with his only daughter and her family. When they moved north to Detroit, however, Finney chose to stay in Indianapolis, since his talents as a commercial artist were suddenly in great demand.

He also took his family by surprise when he took a second wife—his childhood sweetheart—when he was in his eighties. Finney moved with his new bride to West Palm Beach, where he resumed his landscape painting, partly to earn additional income but mainly to entertain himself. "Grandpa Finney said that nobody in his new surroundings had an original idea," my mother adds.

Despite all the cigarettes and hazy midnight hours at his easel, my great-grandfather lived a long and healthful life, dying peacefully at eighty-nine.

His watercolors are signed simply, "R.P. Finney," and I consider myself lucky to have five of them hanging in my sunroom today. My latest acquisition is a tranquil waterfall landscape, which was Finney's wedding gift to my parents. Old "R.P." himself would have been pleased to see how nicely all of his paintings fit with my plants and wicker furnishings.

And he would have been amused to know that one of his works—a Delaware sailboat scene dated 1948—was purchased for sixty dollars by my husband, who was totally surprised when he stumbled upon this treasure six years ago at an antiques shop in downtown Romeo, Michigan. Today the painting is one of our favorite conversation pieces, especially when other artists come to visit.

I have no idea what Finney's watercolor landscapes would be worth on the market today, though they are just as fresh and vibrant as they must have looked when he first painted them. This ancestor left me not only the legacy of his Impressionistic watercolors, but also a deep admiration and respect for people who manage to earn a living, however humble, through their art.

Wedding Song

August 11, 1996

It was, by far, one of the nicest wedding receptions I've ever attended.

The bride wasn't wearing white; the groom wore Bermuda shorts. There was no banquet hall. There were no matchbooks or napkins stamped with "Kathy and Dave, July 26, 1996." No bridesmaids in billowy southern-belle petticoats. No disc jockeys. No tuxedo-clad musicians playing "We've Only Just Begun."

Everything was absolutely perfect. There was prime rib cooking on the grill. Good champagne chilling in coolers. There were new roses on the table and candles flickering in the garden.

And none of the guests at this ingenious reception had even received a wedding invitation. In fact, with few exceptions, most of us had arrived assuming that this was to be a fortieth birthday celebration for Kathy, my brother-in-law's intended. Carrying birthday gifts up the driveway, we all marched triumphantly into Kathy's backyard. But the surprise was on us.

Dave, my husband's brother, and Kathy had stolen away to the local mayor and married secretly that afternoon.

Kathy and Dave had been dating for several years, but always kept quiet about marriage plans. The rest of us just assumed that Kathy was waiting for her two daughters to finish high school, so we didn't ask too many questions. We tried not to pry. But we all hoped Dave and Kathy would eventually marry, since Kathy and her daughters fit so comfortably around our family table.

But back to the surprise wedding reception. I was still shouting "Happy Birthday, Kathy!" when I was handed an official-looking folder containing the newlyweds' marriage certificate—the real reason for the garden party. (My in-laws are still chuckling over my rare moment of speechlessness.)

"We didn't want a big fuss," my new sister-in-law explained as soon as I regained consciousness. "We just wanted everyone to be here to celebrate." Kathy and Dave grinned while their other guests, mostly family, laughed until the tears rolled. There was joy—real joy—on that pretty summer evening.

In retrospect, part of what made the occasion so luminous was the unpretentious beauty and simplicity at the heart of its plan. Dave and Kathy did it their way—without the superfluous frills and lace. It was a gift to their guests.

There's nothing like a sweet surprise to shake up old routines and to remind us that we're here to enjoy the ride. Even ten-year-old Nate, who's too young to understand the complexities of romance, was tickled. "Here I thought I was going to a birthday party," he said. "But I walked away with a new aunt and a bunch of new relatives."

So what do you buy for unpredictable newlyweds who insist they have everything they need and will be spending their honeymoon quietly in Northern Michigan?

Doug and I made them a celebration basket filled with treats to enjoy on a picnic in the woods or by a fire in a cabin. Getting a little carried away, as I tend to do, I added a tiny book of quotations on romantic love. Thumbing through the book before I wrapped it, I found a quote from poet Johann von Schiller, which neatly summed up this whirlwind series of summer events: "I have enjoyed the happiness of the world; I have lived and loved."

Keeping Up
Appearances

Recovering Perfectionist

July 27, 2003

It's just a simple garden plaque, but I knew I had to order one as soon as I saw it in a mail-order catalog. Handcrafted from terra cotta, it announces in plain bold letters: EMBRACE IMPER-FECTION.

I bought it to hang on a brick wall near the patio. But somehow, it looked out of place with the other ceramic plaques my husband and I had collected from summer art fairs. It was a little too perfect and needed some crafty touches—a few dabs of paint here and there to make it look old and weathered. Never one to argue, my artistic husband gave the plaque a nice patina and hung it where I would see it from the garden room window.

Now that I think about it, I should have ordered several to post all over the house.

I've battled perfectionism most of my life, and while it has served me well at times, it usually makes me miserable. Sometimes it makes others miserable, too.

Perfectionism is the snarky little gremlin hissing in my ear when the floors are littered with muddy shoes and old newspapers. It tells me I'm a lousy housekeeper and that I shouldn't even think of entertaining company until everything is spotless. It also reminds me that my table settings never look like the ones in *House & Garden*, anyway.

Perfectionism is the critical woman looking back at me in the mirror—the woman who thinks I need to lose more weight, or that the shirt I am wearing wasn't ironed properly. She reminds me that I will never be as cool as Lauren Hutton.

Perfectionism is the imaginary editor looking over my shoulder while I type. She nags when my sentences are weak, and loves to remind me that I'm *not really* a writer. If I really slip and misspell a word or dangle a modifier in one of my columns or articles, I brood for hours, convinced that my readers have lost faith in me, and that every English teach in Oakland County has ripped my offending piece from the paper and waved it in front of her class. My imaginary editor never lets me forget.

"Perfectionism is the voice of the oppressor, the enemy of the people," warns novelist Anne Lamott. "It will keep you cramped and insane your whole life."

The crazy thing is, I know better. And oddly enough, I've always appreciated quirkiness in other people and the things they own. Distressed furniture, thrift-shop finds, overgrown cottage gardens, non-pedigree pets, freckles and crooked smiles intrigue me. The people whose style I admire tend to be rule-breakers or different drummers. Even the saints were social misfits.

Like most card-carrying perfectionists, I began my career as a people-pleaser. As a kid I was told that if you can't do something exactly right, it's not worth doing at all. Looking for approval from teachers, I never colored outside the lines. As a teen-ager, I dressed to please my peers but avoided upsetting my parents. Finally, by the time I reached my forties, I realized the pursuit of perfection was futile, not to mention exhausting.

To embrace imperfection is to let go of the need to be right, or look good, all of the time. It's never easy. But as Anne Lamott advises, I keep telling myself that messes and mistakes are proof that real life is being lived here. And even when I can't fully embrace imperfection, as my garden plaque urges, I try, at least, to shake hands with it.

When More Isn't Enough

May 14, 1999

S pring is here and FOR SALE signs are sprouting like dandeli-
ons. Several signs have cropped up in our neighborhood, and
each triggers a memory of the time my husband and I decided
to sell the home we owned before the one we live in now.

We lived in our previous home nearly five years—long enough
to know we'd miss our neighbors after the move. But we thought
we'd outgrown it. We needed more storage. The bedrooms were
cramped. And we had to have a bigger kitchen.

Before listing our home on the market, our Realtor asked us to
outline its special features along with any improvements we had
made. The list was very long: New roof, new fence, new landscap-
ing. Air-conditioning. Buckets of paint. Yards of wallpaper. Hours
of elbow grease.

That's when I began to appreciate how nice that home really
was. Suddenly I saw it through the eyes of a prospective buyer who

would fall in love with it. I imagined another woman walking slowly through its rooms, admiring the carved oak mantel in our living room, then moving on to examine the cute vintage tiles in the kitchen. Maybe she wouldn't have chosen the dark print wallpaper in the first-floor bathroom. But surely she'd be pleased to see that the floors upstairs had been refinished. Maybe she could picture her own writing desk in the cozy spare bedroom with the sloped ceiling.

That wasn't the only time I nursed a few regrets about selling the house. And that's when I developed a theory that nobody cleans a home thoroughly until it's time to show it to the public.

The moment a FOR SALE sign is planted on your front lawn, the place is fit for a magazine feature. It smells like Murphy's Oil Soap. The tiniest closets look roomy again (because most of your shoes are stuffed in a box under the bed). Your old stove glistens like it did in the showroom. The front door sports a fresh coat of paint. The whole place wears a brand-new attitude.

So why the heck are you selling it? Unless your boss has transferred you to Boston, or you've suddenly acquired a set of triplets, your reason might have something to do with the fictitious notion that a bigger house will solve most of your problems.

"It is human nature always to want just a little More," writes therapist Timothy Miller, author of *How to Want What You Have: Discovering the Magic and Grandeur of Ordinary Existence* (Avon). "People look for More under the delusion that they will be happy when they get More. In fact, if and when they get More, they are not any happier than they were before, and they still want More."

We can control our appetite for More, he says, by practicing three basic principles: to have compassion for others, to pay attention to the positive things in life, and to feel gratitude for the blessings we already have.

"When you learn to want what you have," Miller writes, "you will start to live in accordance with the old saying that happiness is a way of traveling rather than a destination."

Miller has a point. After reading his book, I've become more grateful for the home I live in—and for all the good things in my life. I'm realizing the fullness of having enough. Any day now, I'll stop dreaming about the extra closet space at Meadow Brook Hall.

———————

Little Black Dress

December 4, 1997

"I am against fashion that doesn't last."
—Coco Chanel

It's been years since I last worried about what to wear to holiday parties. When the occasion calls for something more formal than jeans and a jacket, I reach for one of several black dresses I own. Black wool, black velvet, black silk, black velour...It's good to have a closetful of options.

All women owe a great debt of gratitude to the little black dress, also known as the LBD. With or without pearls, it gets us through business meetings, cocktail parties, concerts, and funerals. It makes us look taller and more sophisticated. It forgives us for all the Halloween candy we ate this fall.

Amy Holman Edelman's *The Little Black Dress* (Simon & Schuster) celebrates the long life of this indelible fashion icon and explores its considerable impact on our culture.

Edelman credits Coco Chanel for popularizing the black cocktail dress in 1926. The famous French designer, she says, liberated women from fussy pastel tea dresses and other Victorian frou-frou. And thanks to improved methods of mass production, the LBD soon became available to almost every woman.

But as Edelman reminds us, black has been making fashion statements throughout the centuries.

"Black is the color most often chosen to cloak the pious," she notes. "It reflects the humility of a nun's habit and the practical endurance of servants and livery." And for ages, respectable black has been worn during long periods of mourning.

It also has a flip side, a darker nature. Black can evoke vampires' capes, witches' robes, suicidal moods, and a delicious penchant for scandal.

Shocking a conservative public in 1884, the most famous black dress in history was worn by Madame Virginie Gautreau in John Singer Sargent's "Madame X." Gautreau, who posed for the portrait in a voluptuous black evening gown, was a married woman of "refined tastes and shadowy reputation"—otherwise known in Paris for her adulterous affairs. At the time, this bad woman in the little black dress almost ruined a painter's career.

Today, the contradictory nature of black—pious and sinful—only adds to its intrigue and enhances its appeal. No wonder it feels right for a big night out on the town.

And there's no denying that black can be bohemian, or downright rebellious, in its refusal to compete with pattern and color. Black is cool by itself. Perhaps for that reason, it dominates the wardrobes of motorcycle gangs, creative types, and other expatriates.

Of course, we have Audrey Hepburn to thank for making black look equally at home in coffeehouses and cocktail bars. After its appearance in *Breakfast at Tiffany's*, Hepburn's black cocktail dress became an everlasting symbol of New York glamour.

Painter Georgia O'Keeffe, also known for her high-spirited individualism, wore a simple black dress at a time when other women thought the look was too harsh. As Edelman points out, O'Keeffe's mentor and husband, the photographer Alfred Stieglitz, was first attracted to the painter "by the distinct nature of her dress."

In the seven decades since its debut, as Edelman notes, the black dress has become a uniform that expresses a modern woman's contradictions and celebrates her independence. It announces that she's dressing for herself.

In a season overburdened by decisions—what to buy for Aunt Beth; what to wear to the office Christmas party—the little black dress offers the ease of simplicity.

Or, as I keep telling my husband, you simply can't own too many.

Brief Thoughts on Thong Underwear

February 22, 2004

"Sometimes the best thing for your look is the piece
you leave behind."
—Cynthia Rowley and Ilene Rozenzweig

I was shopping for new underpants at T. J. Maxx when I realized I'm lagging sadly behind in the lingerie department.

A friend who was born in France tells me that chic French women always pay special attention to what they're wearing underneath their elegant cashmere twin sets and tailored suits. Sexy lingerie, she says, is as fundamental as a set of pearls, and can make you feel like a woman even if you're the only one who knows you're wearing it.

So, a week before Valentine's Day I decided to take a closer look at the racks of thong underwear. Now that I'm nearing fifty, I figured it was my last chance to wear thong underpants. This is as good as my cellulite is going to get.

Being a Fruit of the Loom, cotton briefs kind of gal, I was totally baffled by the options. Of course, I've seen thong underwear (and bathing suit bottoms) in the Victoria's Secret catalog. But I'd never given much thought to thongs, other than to hope my teen-age son doesn't spot many of them roaming the beach.

Inspecting the assortment of lacy minimalist panties—some barely big enough to go around a Barbie doll—I was suddenly hit with an early childhood memory. And I burst out laughing, right there in the lingerie aisle at T.J. Maxx.

Indian underwear!

Remember when you were a kid and your underpants would hike up while you were playing dodgeball or climbing the monkey bars?

For me, that memory dates back to the early 1960s, when most kids got away with being politically incorrect. Back then, we coined the term "Indian underwear" after the cheeky Apache warriors in loincloths who'd creep up behind unsuspecting pioneers in popular westerns. It occurred to me that what fashion editors now refer to as thongs actually evolved from the primitive concept of Indian underwear. What goes around comes around. Retro is cool.

Even in retrospect, though, there was nothing cool about underpants riding up your backside or tugging where they shouldn't tug. Indian underwear felt itchy and gross. Other people made fun of you when they caught you trying to rearrange your twisted underpants.

As much as I appreciate fashion, including pretty lingerie and cool shoes, I often get annoyed at the folks who design things for women.

I know we've come a long way since the era of corsets and bustles, but still, a lot of what is marketed to us is ill-fitting, itchy and overpriced. Not to mention indecent, even on a beach. While there are a few designers putting a practical spin on women's clothing (Eileen Fisher comes to mind), they are rare in an industry that ranks sex over beauty and comfort. Thankfully, lingerie companies like Maidenform still manufacture modest cotton bikinis and comfy briefs for boring old girls like me.

So what about those racy, minimalist thongs?

Well, I left them all on the rack for Barbie and her younger gal pals. After all these years, I decided I've outgrown Native American underpants. And I'm too vain to be caught tugging at my invisible panty line.

Sandal Season

June 6, 2004

N ow that Memorial Day is safely behind us, anyone who follows primeval rules for proper attire can start wearing white shoes whenever the urge strikes.

And who doesn't love the freedom summer brings? When Michigan's weather finally heats up, most of us can walk barefoot on the beach or run errands in shorts and flip-flops. Still, the very thought of flaunting my toes in public is demoralizing, especially since I have trouble finding sandals that flatter me. The bottom line is this: My feet are pitiful. Or so I've been told.

And this is where the column moves from its carefree focus on summer fashion to the topic of careless insults and how they have the power to haunt us forever.

It was Jim, a former college roommate of my husband's, who first pointed out that my toes were radically deformed. Known for his deadpan humor and scorching cynicism, Jim was intellectually gifted. But like the average college kid, Jim didn't realize that his unbridled wit needed to be turned down a notch.

Though it was nearly thirty years ago, I've never forgotten the night a small group of friends, including Jim and my future husband, Doug, decided to play euchre. All of us were sitting in a circle on a shag rug in a cramped dormitory room. Making a fateful mistake, I pulled off my loafers and exposed my bare feet. Jim cut the deck and started dealing the cards.

"My God, look at those FEET," Jim shouted, catching sight of my bare toes. "If I were you, Cindy, I'd never show them to anyone. You should always wear socks!"

Jim was mean but he wasn't wrong. My feet are flat and seriously afflicted with hammer toes, which tend to curl under like eagle talons. Back then, I often wore ill-fitting shoes that also left me with a complete set of painful red corns. Needless to add, I spent the rest of the evening with my feet tucked beneath me.

Thanks, in part, to Jim's sardonic humor, I eventually developed a thicker skin that has served me well. But I still wince every time I have to remove my shoes in public.

A girlfriend tactfully suggested that I see a good podiatrist, or at least try a pedicure, to help me feel more enthused about summer sandals. I've considered it, but I suspect even the best doctor in town would recoil in horror if I were to remove my socks.

Speaking of doctors, I should add that Jim took his verbal cutting edge to medical school and later became a surgeon. I've heard he has since perfected a reassuring bedside manner, and is not performing surgery on people's feet.

My own son, who heads for college this fall, has a razor-sharp sense of humor, too. And despite my objections, he insists that sarcasm is the universal language of young people. I call it verbal abuse.

As a writer and a mother, I've learned that words are powerful tools that can both soothe and repair injuries—and leave indelible scars. I believe that language, written or spoken, should be treated as the precious gift that it is. We all have the right and an obligation to tell our truth, but we must do so carefully.

Humor that hurts or pinches is never funny. The cost of a "joke"—especially one aimed at another person's weak spot—is dangerously high. And I have a closet full of shoes to prove it.

Seeing Red

July 6, 2003

"Is that really your hair?" a reader asked last week in an e-mail. I wasn't sure if he wanted to know if I'm wearing a wig in my photo, or if the color is natural. The hairdo isn't a wig, but the color is chemically enhanced. It's been mine for about eleven years now.

My natural color was light auburn, and I've always had the freckles to match. But eventually the hair turned reddish brown, then grayish brown, then just grayish. So I'm forever indebted to Clairol for giving me an honorary place among the redheads I've always admired, including Lucille Ball and Pippi Longstocking.

I'm not sure why red hair has such a hold on me. Maybe it has to do with my perverse streak.

From Oliver Cromwell to Billy the Kid, redheads have battled a dubious, albeit colorful, reputation. They've been feared and shunned ever since Eric the Red was expelled from Norway for his murderous exploits. Redheads tend to be seen as quick-tempered, unpredictable, promiscuous, flamboyant, and a little wacky.

In movies and novels, they're typically cast as villains, fools, or trolls. Not surprisingly, they've been linked to sorcery and witchcraft. (Remember Endora—Samantha's devious flame-haired mother in the TV series "Bewitched"?)

In ancient Greece, theatrical performers chose black wigs for law-breakers and evil-doers. Blond wigs were used for the good guys and, of course, red wigs for the clowns.

"Hair-color stereotypes seem to be very long lasting," notes Stephen Douglas, author of *The Redhead Encyclopedia* (StoneCastle Literary Group). The book contains more than you'd ever need to know about redheads—scientific data, folklore, plus several lists of famous redheads from movie stars to assorted renegades.

According to Douglas's research, blonds do have more fun, while bright red remains the least popular of all hair hues on the spectrum.

"Blond females were rated significantly more beautiful and feminine than redheaded females," Douglas explains. But things are even worse for carrot-top guys. Blond men were rated as powerful and good-looking, while redheaded males were viewed as "less potent" and even less successful than redheaded women.

A longtime fan of redheads, Douglas reminds us that red hair goes in and out of fashion, and was most popular during eras of "romance and renaissance."

"It becomes almost a challenge to not find a redheaded angel or Madonna in paintings during the period of Raphael," he explains. "Then there are those, regardless of the age, who simply loved red hair, like Titian, Monet and Renoir."

In style or out, I'm convinced that redheads have unique advantages. When Nate was younger, for instance, he found it easier to spot me in a store if he wandered too far away. He surprised me once, calling me a "beacon of light" at the local Kmart. I was touched.

Now that he's a teen-ager and always on the lookout for new nicknames, my red hair is no less inspirational. "Fire Scalp" is what he called me last week.

I like it. Fire Scalp has a poetic, warrior ring to it, sort of like Hagar the Horrible. I've been called worse things.

Thrift Shop Angel

December 21, 2003

"In almost every situation, there are ways that we can fly higher, at fuller wingspan." —Marianne Williamson

T hese days you can't predict the shoppers you'll bump into at your local thrift store. And you probably don't expect to hear the flutter of angel wings amid the racks of used clothing.

Known as one of the regulars, I frequent thrift shops in search of secondhand treasures—the Chanel business suit in mint condition; the Ralph Lauren evening jacket worn only once. Admittedly, I haunt these places not because I need to (though I love a good bargain) but because I'm intrigued by beautiful old clothes. In my holier-than-thou moments, I like to remind people that I'm not a thoughtless slave to fashion, but a link in the recycling chain. And I love the thrill of the hunt.

More often than not, I also rub elbows with shoppers who aren't stalking vintage finds or designer labels from Paris. They are the careful spenders who can't afford to pay top dollar for the latest trends at the malls. Some are looking for warm, practical clothing that won't break the grocery budget, especially during Michigan's frigid winters.

The week after Thanksgiving last year, I visited one of my favorite thrift haunts in search of the perfect pair of broken-in jeans. Perusing a rack of faded khaki and denim, I overheard another customer at the sales register.

"Is this sweater on sale this week?" the shopper asked hopefully, holding up a gently used cashmere sweater in pastel pink. "I'd like this for my daughter for Christmas, but twenty dollars is more than I can spend."

The saleswoman behind the counter looked at the price tag and shook her head kindly. No, the sweater wasn't on sale that week—only the blue tags were half off—and it wouldn't be marked down until next month.

Without missing a beat, another shopper spoke up.

"Please, let me buy that sweater for you," she said. "I woke up today feeling blessed and I want to pass it on."

For a moment the shop stood still, as if everyone in it was momentarily stunned.

It was, after all, a very brave and uncommon thing to do—asking a stranger in need if she'd let you buy her a cashmere sweater to give her daughter.

During the season of giving, most of us gladly donate what we can to local charities or mission projects overseas. It's so much easier to scribble a check to a faceless organization whose needy we will never see. Likewise, staying safely at a distance, we clean out our closets and bundle up our old coats, then drop them in boxes outside the church social hall.

Somewhat reluctantly, the woman who wanted the pink sweater agreed to let the stranger purchase it for her. But her gratitude was palpable, and the whole store seemed to breathe again.

A heartwarming conversation about real-life goodness followed, and before long, the saleswoman and every customer within earshot were fighting tears. I dried my eyes on a pair of vintage Calvins I'd uncovered.

Composing myself, I walked up to the counter, hoping for closer look at the generous soul who'd just bought a cashmere sweater for someone she'd never met. I wanted to thank her for rekindling the holiday spirit I thought I'd lost in the seasonal frenzy of shopping and baking.

But like most angels, she'd flitted out the door as quietly as she'd arrived—most likely, on her way to another miracle.

———————————

Keeping the Seasons

Ordinary Days Deserve Our Best

May 10, 1999

"It's a funny thing about life; If you refuse to accept anything but the best, you very often get it." —Somerset Maugham

"Oh look, you're using your good china," my mom said as we gathered at my table for dinner.

The holidays were long past and there were no anniversaries or birthdays to toast, which is why Mom was so surprised to see my grandmother's gold-rimmed dishes and goblets gleaming by candlelight on an otherwise ordinary evening.

I'm not by nature a fussy hostess, and excessive formality makes me nervous. Over the years, my mother and other family members have gotten used to being served on casual ceramic dinnerware—or even on leftover paper plates stamped with birthday balloons and purple dinosaurs.

So why the fine china?

I think it's because I'm getting philosophical in my middle age. Why save my best dinnerware for company or so-called special occasions? Doesn't my family deserve to enjoy the nicest things we own?

Likewise, why reserve good clothes for special occasions? If you're like me, you have at least one terrific outfit you're saving for a time when you'll be invited to some momentous affair—maybe a banquet at the White House or a reception at the Vatican. Outfits like this droop on their hangers, unworn for years, until they go out of style and end up at a local resale shop. Meanwhile, we spend most of our time in sloppy jeans and sweats. After all, our best friends and family love us as we are, and it isn't as if Harrison Ford is going to ring the doorbell.

You've doubtless heard the popular catchphrase, "Life isn't a dress rehearsal," which is printed on everything from inspirational posters to shopping bags. But there's poignant truth in it. Good china and candles aren't just for fancy dinner parties: We should use them to honor and brighten our everyday meals. And we ought to at least try to look nice for the people whose homes and lives we share. There's little merit in saving our best for a precious event that might never happen.

This occurred to me last week when I reorganized my files and found an old birthday card I'd bought for my dad not long before he died. "I'm so glad you're my father," it began in sentimental, greeting-card prose. Because I missed the chance to give that card to my dad, it has remained unsigned in a drawer for more than four years. But I still can't manage to throw it away.

While browsing in an antiques shop recently, I found a charming Quimper plate that would fit perfectly in my mother's collection. (Had I been looking for it, of course, it wouldn't have been there.) So I bought it on the spot, knowing full well that I wasn't going to save it for her birthday or Mother's Day. Those occasions seemed too far off in the nebulous future, and I wanted Mom to enjoy her gift right away. Later that afternoon, I drove to her house and gave her the plate—without ceremony, wrapping, or ribbon.

It could have been just another uneventful Saturday on my calendar. But it felt like a real celebration.

October Memories

October 12, 1998

L ately I've been thinking of these lines from Anne Mary
  Lawler's poem about the seasons:

October dresses in flame and gold,
Like a woman afraid of growing old.

This is a potent month for memories. Yesterday I watched while
my son and the children next door tumbled like acrobats in the fallen
leaves. (Is there a kid in the Midwest who hasn't done this?) And
later in the evening, I sniffed the familiar aroma of wood-burning
fires, another indisputable sign that winter is on its way.

For me, the smoky scents of October always evoke a favorite
memory of my father raking leaves in the small backyard of our first
home. That memory is more than three decades old, but it glows as
vividly as the logs crackling in the grate tonight.

When I was growing up—before environmental laws—everyone in my neighborhood raked leaves into neat brown piles, then
burned them near the curb or in backyard bonfires. Dry and brittle
as bones, the leaves snapped furiously when introduced to a match.
Back then, October weekends seemed to drift in mysterious clouds
of gray-blue smoke—the perfect prelude to Houdini's Halloween.

Like most fathers, mine worked on weekdays, and often spent

his weekends doing yard work. Long before the term "quality time" was coined by childcare experts, Dad would enlist my help raking leaves on Sunday after church. I offered very little assistance, preferring to toss his neatly piled leaves back into the air, or to roll in what remained of his handiwork. Regardless, he seemed to enjoy my reckless company—and I enjoyed the novelty of helping him. Unlike my mom, who would have seized the opportunity for "girl talk," my dad didn't always communicate with words. On those brisk autumn afternoons, with the sun glinting through bare branches of oak and maple, it was enough for us to *be* together. He raked, I rolled, and nothing of dire importance was ever said.

Still, young as I was, I felt the ancient ache and pull of October.

By then, I understood the seasons were cyclical; that the easy days of summer would return as surely as apples had ripened every fall. But I'd also begun to grasp the concept that time trudges ahead in a straight line, like it or not, ruffling the smooth texture of our days as it marches forward. I couldn't have explained it quite this way, but suddenly I knew I'd have to "yield with a grace," as Robert Frost once wrote, "the end of a love or a season."

I recall watching my handsome young father in his plaid flannel shirt while he whistled and tended his banks of smoldering leaves, their acrid smoke filling my nostrils and forcing tears. I remember wishing that everything could stay the same—that I wouldn't have to grow up or grow old; that autumn afternoons wouldn't bleed to winter.

It was as if I had glimpsed the distant future and seen my father's empty chair at our Thanksgiving table.

Of course, Dad had no idea that I had stumbled on a vast, disturbing truth and was forever changed by it. He worked contentedly, pausing only to watch me or to loosen the dried leaves from the long teeth of his rake.

And that is the way I like to remember him: arrested in time on that October afternoon, living in the moment, always whistling.

Why I Still Love Halloween

October 16, 2004

Halloween always stirs a delicious caldron of memories. Baby boomers are a nostalgic bunch, and most of us can recall at least one costume we wore in grade school. Wearing yards of pink tulle and a homemade foil crown, I dressed up as Miss America when I was in the first grade in 1960. And who could forget trick-or-treating in packs until our pillowcases were too heavy to lug around the block?

While the holiday suffered a lull in the 1970s, the "season of the witch" now competes with Christmastime as the biggest party season of the year. And with all due respect to religious groups refusing to celebrate it, I never thought of Halloween as inherently evil. What most people seem to enjoy about the holiday is the creativity factor.

Stepping over age limits, Halloween extends an open invitation to play dress-up. It inspires us to raid attics and local thrift shops for the most outlandish outfits we can jumble together. If only for one magical night, it gives us permission to drop the dull disguise of conformity.

For wardrobe junkies like me, Halloween is reason enough to hoard pieces of vintage clothing and jewelry that, by all rights, should have been donated to charity ages ago. My husband now refers to our attic as "the clothing museum," and with good reason. Friends who have trouble rustling up an outfit will often call for help during dress-up emergencies. ("Can I borrow one of your medieval jester hats for a clown costume?" is not an unusual request.) Over the years, in fact, I've collected so many crazy hats that we have to store them in a large steamer trunk behind the living room couch. Those hats get the most wear near Halloween, when even the most reserved engineer who visits will try on a pith helmet or a plumed pirate hat and wear it to the dinner table.

And why not? Historically speaking, the holiday has always been a celebration of the harvest, a madcap prelude to the more dignified ceremonials of Thanksgiving.

Halloween's roots weave back more than 2,000 years to the early Celts of Ireland, Scotland, and Wales. It was originally known as the festival of Samhain, according to Caitlin Matthews, a Celtic scholar and author of *The Celtic Book of Days* (Destiny Books). The festival, she explains, marked the end of the farming season and the beginning of the Celtic new year. Lavish banquet tables were prepared for the ancestors, who were believed to pierce the veil between the living and the dead on the eve of Samhain. It was also time to rekindle the bonfires that would sustain the clans in winter.

"In the Christian era," Matthews writes, "the festival was reassigned to the Feast of All Saints; however, many of the customs surrounding modern Halloween still concern this ancient understanding of the accessibility of the dead."

And we can thank our Irish immigrants for the jack-o'-lantern, which reputedly wards off evil spirits. This custom evolved from the old practice of carving out large turnips and squash, then illuminating them with candles. The term jack-o'-lantern was derived from a folk tale involving a crafty Irishman named Jack, who outwitted the Devil.

On cool autumn nights, when the moon is bright and leaves scatter nervously across the sidewalk, a bittersweet chill runs up and down my spine.

Like my Celtic ancestors, I'm moved to take stock of how much I've accomplished throughout the year, and how many things I've left undone. My to-do list is yards long. There are parts of the world I haven't seen; stories I haven't written; debts and favors to repay. I marvel at the mellow beauty of the season, which has always been my favorite, but also feel a little sad that one more year is drawing to its close.

All said and done, I like to think of Halloween as the big goodbye party we throw for autumn. All in good fun.

———————————

Feasting by Candlelight

December 14, 2003

"Let parents bequeath to their children not riches,
but the spirit of reverence." —Plato

It was the weirdest thing. A pair of brass candlesticks I'd kept on top of the curio cabinet had suddenly disappeared. It was the night before Thanksgiving, and up until then, I was living under the delusion that everything was in fairly good order. My dining room table was polished and set with cloth napkins and my Grandmother's china.

But after putting the final touch on my centerpiece, I noticed the two candlesticks were missing. They weren't the ones I'd planned to use—but their absence was a real mystery. Doug swore he hadn't seen them, and our son Nate was out with friends that evening.

I'll never know what possessed me to go outside and look through Nate's car, but I did. There, in a small box on the front seat, were the kidnapped candlesticks plus a pair of partially burned black candles leftover from Halloween.

Why on earth would a high-school senior have these items stashed in his car? I could hardly wait for the explanation.

Well, the candlestick thief returned home shortly thereafter, followed by a noisy troop of teen-agers. All were in good spirits and looking forward to their long holiday weekend. To my surprise, the topic of the evening was the traditional Thanksgiving meal they had shared that same afternoon in the high-school cafeteria. The feast had been their own idea, in fact, with no prompting from teachers or school administrators. Few parents even knew they'd planned it.

One student brought a large roasted turkey; others brought side dishes, tablecloths, and trimmings. Nate's contribution to the feast was—you guessed it—the pair of candlesticks with the half-burned Halloween candles, which he'd grabbed in his usual rush out the door that morning.

"Why didn't you tell me?" I grilled him. "I would have given you some new candles." I reminded him, too, that he shouldn't remove things from our dining room without asking. To his credit, Nate apologized, and then informed me that he'd grabbed the "ugliest, most hideous pair of candlesticks" he could find, to avoid upsetting me.

Hideous candlesticks aside, teen-agers never cease to amaze and delight me. Just when you wonder if they'd even care about ceremonial things like candlelight and holiday dinners, they turn the tables on you. That Thanksgiving feast in the cafeteria was one of the last Nate and his friends would celebrate as the extended family they've become. Like all families, biological or adopted, they were sharing a ritual as ancient as recorded history. Feasting together provides comfort and forges lifelong memories.

It also occurred to me that my candlestick thief is one lucky young man, especially since he's an only child, to have grown up with other youngsters who'd bother to create a holiday meal together. Last week, in fact, another parent told me that the kids enjoyed it so much that they hoped to do something equally festive for Christmas and Easter.

"Family ritual is pretty much anything we do together deliberately, as long as it's juiced up with some flourish that lifts it above humdrum routine," notes Meg Cox, author of *The Book of New Family Traditions* (Running Press). As Cox points out, anthropologists have yet to discover a human culture that didn't practice rituals. Rituals impart a sense of identity and help us navigate change. Even the simplest routines we practice when our children are very young, in fact, will help them feel grounded and secure.

So it's definitely worth the trouble—using your Grandma's silver, setting a nice table, and recreating holiday menus that have special meaning to your family.

Dress up for the occasion and memorize a toast. And always be sure to keep extra candlesticks on hand.

The Other Side of the Kettle

December 6, 1998

It's the Friday after Thanksgiving, and ordinarily I'd be sleeping late. But today I'm joining the corps of community volunteers who ring bells to collect holiday donations for the local Salvation Army. I have an hour to shower, dress, and drive to the Oakland Mall, where my thirteen-year-old and I will be stationed.

This will be our first time out as bell ringers. I'd like to feel noble about the whole thing, but truthfully, I'm a little nervous.

9:45 A.M.: Nate and I arrive at the mall, which is already buzzing with holiday shoppers. We pick up our red kettle and brass bells, then head to our assigned post at the Hudson's entrance facing Fourteen Mile Road. Luckily, the day is unseasonably warm, which will make our three-hour shift so much easier.

10:00: At first we feel a bit silly, ringing bells to get people to put money in the kettle. Worse yet, few shoppers are responding. Some people whip out their cell phones and start chatting as soon as they notice us, maybe to avoid making eye contact. Others pick up their pace as they pass us. It occurs to me that it might help to smile at these people. I ask Nate if he wants to sing some upbeat holiday carols. Wouldn't "Jingle Bells" would work nicely in this situation?

"No, Mom," he hisses back. "You're scaring people."

10: 45: To relieve boredom, I practice paying attention. With the clear focus of a Zen master, I count how many shoppers are wearing leather coats. I spot a dark blue limousine cruising slowly through the lot, and beyond, scores of shiny SUVs jockeying for parking spaces. And for the first time, I notice the Salvation Army slogan posted above our kettle. It reads: "Need has no season."

11:00: Things are definitely picking up. Several generous shoppers are reaching into their purses or pockets. A few pause long enough to push several dollar bills through the kettle slot. We're on a roll.

11:10: Looks like we're finally getting the hang of bell ringing. To keep things interesting, we try to vary the rhythms: Ting-ta-ting-ta-TING...Ting-ting-TING. We've also found that it's less irritating when we don't ring the bells simultaneously, or when we ease up and tinkle them gently.

11:15: I am desperate to go to the bathroom. Nate will man the kettle alone while I take a break.

11:30: Nate tells me he collected "a lot more money" while I was gone, and is looking very pleased with himself.

11:45: Uh-oh. Three husky teen-aged boys, jeans sagging below their hips, approach the kettle. They do not look like honor-roll students. They are not smiling. I muster my courage, fully expecting a little holiday harassment. But I'm a rotten judge of character. The tallest one stuffs a five-dollar bill into the kettle, then mumbles "Merry Christmas" before shuffling into Hudson's with his buddies.

12:00 P.M.: It's almost impossible to predict who will give and who won't. A few shoppers mumble something about giving at the office. Well-dressed, middle-aged couples seem less inclined to contribute. Yet a surprising number of young people—teen-agers in particular—stop to push their folded dollars through the kettle slot. Then there are the sad-eyed folks who apologize because they can't give more. We tell them sincerely that every penny counts.

12:40: I should have known we wouldn't escape the Grinch. Stopping two inches in front of me, a hefty, mean-spirited guy with cigarette breath demands to know "exactly who gets their hands on the money in that kettle."

I try to explain the exemplary work of the Salvation Army. I explain how the money collected will go into social programs serving hundreds of needy families, homeless people, senior citizens, and countless others who need help in our community—not only at Christmas, but throughout the year.

The Grinch tosses a few coins into the kettle, and then stalks away toward the crowded parking lot.

"Happy holidays," I shout after him. Happy holidays, just the same.

The Waiting Season

December 13, 2003

One of my favorite seasons, Advent is a time of waiting and anticipation—a time when it feels as if something truly awesome is about to unfold.

For most Christian churches, it marks the beginning of the liturgical year. Advent starts on the fourth Sunday before Christmas Day—the Sunday closest to November 30—and ends on Christmas Eve. If Christmas Eve falls on a Sunday, it is then counted as the fourth Sunday of Advent. In many churches, a ceremonial candle is lighted near the altar every week during the season.

I still remember my first Advent calendar. A simple cardboard model, it was sprinkled with gold and silver glitter and had tiny perforated windows to be opened daily until Christmas. Behind each window was a small illustration associated with the Nativity in Bethlehem—an angel with a trumpet, a Wise Man, or a shepherd with a lamb.

My best friend in grade school was a devout Catholic and a seasoned authority on the proper use of Advent calendars. As she often reminded me, the perforated windows were meant to be opened *only* on their designated days. Sneaking a peak at the future was strictly prohibited.

Being a practical Presbyterian at the time, I could see nothing sinful in staying ahead of schedule. And by the second week of Advent, I knew what was behind every door and window, including the largest and final one that revealed the baby Jesus. Once I did this, of course, I'd completely spoiled my own fun. Half the beauty of any Advent calendar, after all, is the magical sense of wonder and anticipation it provides. If nothing else, I'd learned a small lesson in patience—or how to wait gracefully.

"Most of us think of waiting as something very passive," writes Catholic theologian Henri Nouwen in "Waiting for God," an essay on Advent. "Active waiting means to be fully present to the moment, in the conviction that something is happening where you are and that you want to be present to it."

My own son's birthday also falls during Advent. Nate just turned eighteen last week—a landmark birthday that got me thinking about patience, grace, seasons, and the incredible journey of motherhood.

A senior year in high school now, Nate is over six feet tall and diligently preparing for college. Every day after school he makes a beeline to the mailbox, hoping to find acceptance letters from the various universities he's applied to. He is in a waiting mode, too, anticipating a bright and challenging future.

My duties as a parent often feel paradoxical. I must help my child feel grounded and secure, yet loosen my maternal grip a little more each year. And like most parents, I often try to imagine what the future holds. I want some assurance that my boy will be safe, happy, and fully capable of managing on his own. But it's not for me to know what's behind every door or window to his future.

The only thing I have for certain is the moment at hand, a moment to be seized and cherished. It's another lesson in patience for me—one little window at a time.

Hope Shines in a
Dark Season

December 23, 2001

"Faith could be called a kind of whistling in the dark."
—Frederick Buechner

Three years ago, I decorated my kitchen window with a set of miniature white lights. I don't recall where I got the idea, but I wound those tiny lights around a yard of silk grapevine leaves and the effect was magical. It cheered me up on the gloomiest winter evenings.

I enjoyed the lights so much, in fact, that I never took them down. As far as I know, there's no law that bans twinkle lights beyond the Christmas season.

Besides, I've always had an uneasy relationship with Christmas. I love its essence, the holy message at its core, but I don't like the way we've commercialized it. And this year, especially, Christmas seems more like a bizarre intrusion than a holiday. Still reeling from September 11, the whole country is in a recovery mode.

Locally, it's harder to feel festive because of a young man named

Scott, an athletic high-school student who died December 9 after a long, unfathomable illness.

I didn't know Scott personally. But I know Scott's mother, Lynette, because our children have attended the same schools since kindergarten. Everyone in this community admired Lynette's grace and strength while Scott lingered in a coma at the hospital. We all kept track of his progress, and we all prayed night and day that he'd recover and return to baseball games and high-school dances.

His death at seventeen, so unfair and inexplicable, and so close to Christmas, left a hole the size of Colorado in our hearts. But Scott's passing also served as a lesson in need of review: Our stay on Earth is unpredictable and we must savor the gift of every hour we're given.

So, ready or not, Christmas comes on Tuesday. It's hanging like a star above our heads or a burden on our backs, depending on how we choose to see it. Or, as Anne Lamott wrote, "We must remind ourselves that you can only see the stars when it is dark, and the darker it is, the brighter the light breaking through."

I remembered this while sitting in an Advent meditation service a few evenings ago. I hadn't been to church in a while; my recent hip replacement surgery had worked as an excuse to avoid getting up early on Sunday mornings.

But after I settled into place in the sanctuary, which was decorated with greens for the season and softly lit with candles, it occurred to me that lately I'd been preoccupied with fear and suffering—my own and everyone else's. Ever since September 11, I felt as if I'd been wandering around the living room with the lights turned off, wondering why I kept tripping on all the furniture. So I asked God to help me rekindle a small light, just a glimmer of Christmas spirit, in my closed heart. Then I went home.

Later, I plugged in the white twinkle lights around my kitchen window. I began a mental list of the miracles that have glimmered through recent crises, local and national.

I recalled the loving support of my family and friends, the skill

of my orthopedic surgeon, the generosity of neighbors and parishio-
ners who bake casseroles for grieving families like Scott's, the hero-
ism of rescue teams at Ground Zero, and the valor of mothers who
lose children but never lose faith. The list went on.

Then I understood.

For all we've endured, we have every reason to sustain hope. We
need the hopeful message of Christmas all year long, and maybe a
small string of white lights to remember it.

———————————

A Light to Warm Our Winter

December 24, 1998

Over the centuries, Christmas has been reinvented and re-packaged, promoted and pummeled, like the cookie dough we cut into festive shapes and decorate every year in December. Christmas is a mass of contradictions.

The day was chosen to honor the birth of a king in a lowly manger—a king who ultimately advocated a life of humility and charity. Yet today the holiday is celebrated more as a buying frenzy than as the birthday of a humble messiah.

Then again, Christmas is a mirror reflecting our culture.

As author Bill McKibben explains in *Hundred Dollar Holiday* (Simon and Schuster), "Christmas has been, and always will be, a product of its time, shaped to fit the particular needs of people, society, and faith in particular moments of history. And nowhere is that clearer than at the very beginning."

Historians can't certify the exact date of Christ's birth. Ironically, Christians decreed in the fourth century that the Feast of the

Nativity would be observed December 25—originally a pagan holiday. The date was deliberately selected to replace the rowdy winter solstice festivals held in those days. On the old Julian calendar, December 25 was the longest night of the year, which partly explains why the torch-carrying pagans had chosen it to glorify the sun.

As church leaders hoped, Christianity eventually took root, and by the end of the thirteenth century, most Europeans celebrated the birth of Jesus. But the pagan aspects of Christmas never were completely snuffed out.

Today, the weeks between Thanksgiving and New Year's serve as an extended invitation to indulge our national craving for activity and entertainment. We've forgotten that the sentimental Christmas we long for, as McKibben explains in his book, evolved during the 1840s when Americans "were mostly poor, worked with their hands, and lived with large, extended families." Today it would be impossible to re-create such a Christmas in suburban America.

"More and more, that old Christmas finally feels played out," McKibben writes. If we've grown ambivalent about the holiday—or even disappointed in it—that's partly why.

Still, at its heart, Christmas remains a celebration of light's triumph over darkness. A celebration of miracles.

Light is also the enduring symbol of Hanukkah, the annual Jewish festival that coincides with the Christian holiday season. Hanukkah marks the rededication of the Temple of Jerusalem and the ceremonial oil that burned miraculously for eight days. With the ritual lighting of the menorah at its core, Hanukkah prevails as a tribute to religious freedom.

It's sobering to remember, especially now, that many people still struggle for the right to worship as they choose. In Ireland, the Middle East, and other parts of the world, many have lost their lives in the names of conflicting gods or warring denominations. Even here, in our own community, we're not totally free of violence, poverty, hunger or hypocrisy. We know it's not enough to donate last year's coats to the poor, or to serve meals at a soup kitchen, but we still haven't figured out how to solve the dilemma of our homeless and needy. And our personal difficulties pale in comparison.

Yet Christmas can be, to borrow from Luke 1:79, "a lamp to give light to those who sit in darkness."

So tonight we rekindle the embers of our faith.

Like pagan revelers, we build fires and throw one last party before surrendering to winter's chill. Like hopeful Magi, we track the glimmer of a distant star, trusting there is something wondrous and good at the end of our most difficult journey. We plug in the lights on the Christmas tree and leave the porch light on for Santa. In church, we light the last candle of Advent to invoke the Divine.

And we still believe in miracles.

––––––––––––

Father's Day

E leven years ago, when my father died, one of the first things my mother and I did was hire a bagpiper to play at his funeral.

He was the son of Scottish immigrants who came to Detroit from the Orkney Islands in the 1920s. Always proud of his Celtic heritage, my dad been raised to appreciate everything about the old country—food, folklore, history. Naturally, he loved the highland bagpipes, and we'd all have to stop whatever we were doing to listen to the pipe-and-drum corps whenever they marched in parades or on television.

The piper we hired for Dad's funeral played a few solemn airs before the interment. I'd requested "Amazing Grace" and "Scotland the Brave"—not very original, I know, but my father loved those pieces, and we all felt better knowing they were the last played before his burial. It was foggy and rainy that morning—very British—

and every somber note from those pipes seemed to linger in the humid July air.

After the funeral, our whole family drifted through our own mental fog. We kept busy driving to banks and government offices to revise my parents' accounts and personal papers. We opened Dad's closet and somehow managed the task of sorting through his suits and ties.

Trying to maintain a normal family routine, Mom and I took Nate, then six, to a local park for a picnic supper. We'd barely unpacked the potato salad when we heard the unmistakable drone of a bagpipe a few feet behind our picnic table. To say we were stunned would be an understatement. And when the piper began playing "Scotland the Brave," well, suffice to say that the tears rolled nonstop, nudging us out of our numbness and into the next stage of healing.

The piper wasn't a phantom, of course, but a very real student who'd decided to practice in the park at the same time we'd chosen to have a summer picnic. But somehow I felt certain that the impromptu recital was a signal from my dad—a mystical "thank you" for the proper sendoff we'd given him a few days earlier.

The piper episode came to mind again this spring, after a beautiful memorial service for the father of a close friend, John.

John's dad was a Navy captain, and the whole family was proud of his military career. John wrote a heartfelt eulogy that celebrated his father's life as a patriotic American and a dedicated father. But even more remarkable, to me, was the fact that John was able to stand at the pulpit and read what he'd written. It was a very brave thing to do, and I have no doubt "The Captain" was saluting John from his new tour of duty in heaven.

Not long after his dad died, John took a business trip to Chicago, where he happened to catch a glimpse of a Navy captain on a street corner.

A longtime newspaper editor, John has never been particularly sentimental or superstitious. But he told me he found comfort in the sight of the familiar Navy uniform and believed it was a sign. He stopped to chat with the captain, briefly telling him about his father's passing. Returning home that evening, he felt more at peace.

As John reminded me later, you don't often spot a Navy captain standing casually on a street corner. Nor is it common to hear a bagpiper droning a few tunes in a suburban park.

No matter how old you are, it's never easy to lose your dad. You keep looking for traces of him wherever you go.

———————

Survival Guide for Grads

May 16, 2004

"I always pass along good advice. It is the only thing to do with it, since it is never of any use to oneself."
—Oscar Wilde

It's graduation season. In keeping with tradition, proud parents, mentors, and elected officials will pass along pithy words of wisdom and advice to students who'll be starting college or launching new careers. To all our local graduates of 2004, I send my very best wishes for your future. Meanwhile, here's a peek at the survival tips I'll be packing in my son's suitcase when he leaves for college this fall.

- Relationships, like cars, need regular upkeep. Maintain the good friendships you've made.

- Learn from your adversaries. The people who push our buttons tend to reflect qualities we dislike in ourselves.

- Dress appropriately for every occasion.

- Encourage others to talk about themselves. You'll make a great first impression and learn something new.

- If you settle for less, that's exactly what you'll get.

- Don't be too proud to ask for help when you need it.

- The notion that everyone is having a better time somewhere else is one of the world's dumbest illusions. Refuse to believe it.

- Losing is a great character builder. If your best effort misses the mark, ask yourself what you can learn from the loss.

- Choose a career you can be proud to list on every form you'll have to fill out.

- Remember Mom's e-mail address.

- Be a community builder. If we can't make peace with our neighbors, there's no hope for the rest of the world.

- It can be lonely at the top. Be careful not to alienate loved ones while achieving your goals.

- Be thoughtful. Good manners were designed to make others feel comfortable and respected.

- Strive for decency and accept nothing less from everyone you hang out with.

- Get enough sleep.

- Make good on your word. Show up on time. If you promised to bring the dessert or move furniture, follow through.

- Keep your faith, but learn about the great religions of the world. Never publicly criticize someone's religious beliefs. Self-righteousness is a huge turn-off.

- Stay in shape; enjoy a recreational sport.

- Spend time alone. Creative ideas and solutions are sparked in solitude.

- Never leave your underwear on the floor. As every good roommate will tell you, neatness is essential in cramped spaces.

- Don't wait for holidays to tell people how much you appreciate them.

- Read for pleasure.

- Always take the high road. Admit your blunders and apologize if you've hurt someone.

- Return what you borrow.

- Go easy on the junk food. Pay attention to what you eat, where it came from, and why you're eating it.

- Find your inner compass and stop seeking approval from others. Be too busy to wonder what other people think of you.

- Spend time outdoors. A walk in the woods is the best antidepressant.

- Never buy an expensive item on impulse. Wait at least a day to ensure you really need it and can afford to pay for it.

- Splurge on comfortable shoes.

- Don't limit your shopping to chain stores. Support local businesses and discover the heart and soul of every new location.

- Travel is the best way to learn about the world, but stay on the lookout for a place to set down roots.

- Obey the speed limit and use turn signals. Steer clear of road rage.

- Savor your memories but don't live in the past. Anyone who insists their high-school or college years were "the best" is stuck in a rut. Life gets richer and juicier as you move on. Enjoy every minute.

Big Fat Weddings

June 5, 2004

I t must be June. Bridal magazines are stacked higher than five-layer wedding cakes at the local newsstands. And everyone, regardless of ethnic background, seems to be planning another Big Fat Greek Wedding.

I'm astounded at how much money, time, and effort it takes to stage a wedding these days—and how little goes into mapping a course for a real marriage.

Over the years, Doug and I have watched newly engaged couples spend months selecting elaborate floral arrangements, inspecting menus from caterers, auditioning professional musicians, and outfitting enough bridal attendants to cast a chorus line on Broadway. The final productions often rivaled the grandest pageants of British nobility. (For all that fuss, I wish I could pretend I was truly touched or impressed.)

But the classiest and most memorable weddings I've attended, in fact, were relatively small and simple—like the sweet garden party my brother-in-law and his bride hosted for the immediate family a few years ago.

Sadly, modest receptions are few and far between.

A neighbor who's planning a late-summer wedding for his son recently shared a link to the Wedding Gazette, which includes a new survey from *Bride's* magazine. According to this study, the "average" wedding in the Midwest runs about $19,000 for 200 guests and five bridal attendants. (But take heart, Mom and Dad: Bridal couples in the New York Metro area typically spend over $31,000.) Ironically, the average cost for the chapel and clergy is—at a mere $232— almost the smallest expense on the list. The bill for the limousine service totals $393, while the florist collects about $756. Estimated at $7,635, a banquet reception is the biggest splurge.

Despite the trend toward extravagant weddings, nearly half of all American marriages end in divorce, the gloomiest statistic of all.

So what snags the wedding lace?

Faithful consumers that we are, we invest way too much energy showering newlyweds with gifts from an upscale bridal registry. Neglecting to counsel them on the sanctity and seriousness of the marriage commitment, we throw them a huge party and hope for the best. Then we wring our hands because so many couples break up before their new washing machines break down.

Observing the sturdiest couples I know, I believe every successful marriage is built on a solid foundation of friendship, faith, and shared vision, not merely the same mattress. As the old saying goes, love is blind but marriage restores its sight. And when the honeymoon is over, the average couple will face tougher dilemmas than where to stash the new bath towels and yard tools.

For better or for worse, there will be career upheaval and financial hassles ahead. Not to mention a child or two. Who will work (or stay home) if they have kids? Who will cook dinner? Do yard work? Scrub toilets? Organize the carpool? Whose relatives will come for Thanksgiving?

My advice to lovebirds is to plan a modest wedding reception and bank the extra cash for a rainy day. Spend less time fretting over what to list on the bridal registry and more time working toward a durable union. Consider prenuptial counseling in addition to Waterford crystal stemware.

Your real challenge, after all, will be to weather life's inevitable storms, long after the bridal gardenias have wilted and the $756 florist bill has been paid.

The Lost Art of Loafing

July 18, 2004

T he sad reality always hits us mid-July: Summer is at the half-
way mark.

Taking inventory of what we've done since June, we realize
how precious little time we've spent relaxing. Wasn't there a song
about "the lazy, hazy days" of summer?

For me, the first half of June exploded like a bottle rocket into
thin air. When I wasn't planning Nate's high-school graduation party,
I was attending parties for other terrific kids. The whole season, in
fact, ballooned with joyful events and ceremonies, including a couple
of weddings, which is why it seems as if we've all been riding an
emotional roller coaster non-stop.

Before summer packs up its beach bag and clears out for a new
school term, I'd like to indulge in a few non-eventful pleasures. Many
Europeans, for example, take the entire month of July or August as
vacation time. While such a long holiday isn't possible for industri-

ous Americans, I'd like to borrow a shorter page from a Parisian friend. *Joie de vivre* isn't complicated, she says, but you have to make time for it.

Here's the plan.

Guilt-free, I'm going to chill out for a week and remember how the words "summer" and "freedom" used to hang together when I was a kid.

With or without a hammock, I'm going to watch more sunsets, spot fireflies, nap with my cats, and contemplate my world by moonlight.

I'll brush up on the names of wild birds and constellations.

Instead of pulling weeds or pruning, I'll sit back and admire what I've planted.

With or without company coming, I'll cut fresh flowers for the dinner table. At least once, I'll steam corn on the grill and make lemonade from scratch.

Heading for the beach with my family, I'll hunt for Petoskey stones, skipping stones, beach glass, and perfect pieces of driftwood. Maybe I'll organize a group to float downriver in tubes. Later, if I can stay awake, I'll go for a midnight swim.

If I can remember the right titles, I'll rent videos of movie classics I haven't watched in ages.

Just for one afternoon, I'll read a novel that has no redeeming social value while I sunbathe without fretting about skin cancer.

I'll ride my bike for an entire morning without checking my watch. After pedaling around a local park, I'll rest under a thick canopy of trees and admire the view.

Most of us schedule our lives too tightly, then rely on "nostalgic flashbacks" to appreciate blissful moments, says Veronique Vienne in *The Art of the Moment: Simple Ways to Get the Most from Life* (Clarkston Potter).

"As you embrace the here and now, don't be surprised if you suddenly feel lucky—lucky to be blessed with a good mind, lucky to have friends who love you for who you are," Vienne advises. "The ultimate gift of the moment is a deep sense of gratitude for simply being alive."

It's always fun to anticipate and celebrate the major milestones. But we need a break from "special" events, not to mention a reprieve from all the speeches about beginnings and endings. We need ordinary time.

Come August, I want to say good-bye to summer knowing that I've squeezed every last drop of its sweetness and savored it all.

———————————

Older and Wiser

One More Year

August 31, 2003

L ately it seems as if I've swallowed summer in one big gulp, like the last swig of Long Island iced tea on a scorching afternoon. I wish I had more in my glass.

I turned forty-nine this month, and already I'm wondering how to make forty-nine last as long as I can possibly stretch it. I plan to age gracefully—no dragging my heels into my fifties. I'd like to become one of those plucky old women who wear purple and "learn to spit," as the Jenny Joseph poem goes. But not so fast.

Recently, Nate and I were having a mock philosophical discussion about the velocity of time. He was anxious for the new family car we'd ordered, which had been delayed in production. To him, the days weren't accelerating fast enough; time was stalling like a faulty engine. Later he complained that summer break was ending too quickly.

His senior year of high school started last week, and I'm still trying to wrap my mind around that idea, too. We've been shopping for colleges since May, and applications will be mailed soon.

Just one more year.

Another mom, whose only child is my son's age, also tastes the bittersweet tang in this last swig of summer. Our lives will change too, she reminds me, when high school ends.

This will be the last year we rush to nuke meals in time for play rehearsals and tennis games.

This will be the last year we quit work early to snag front-row seats at concerts and award banquets.

This will be the last year we snap photos of our kids in tuxedos and prom dresses. And the last year for school uniforms, bagged lunches, bake sales, teachers' luncheons, fund-raisers, permission slips, and field trips.

Of course, there's the sweet ring of freedom in all of this, too. Don't think it hasn't occurred to every middle-aged mother who stands teary-eyed on the same threshold.

I chose to work at home when Nate was younger, combining freelance writing with Tiger Cubs and carpooling. Later on, I tried to stay involved in high-school activities. Meanwhile, I've put a few dreams on hold, not to mention the career goals I've filed away. I've looked forward to the time when I can start my day without checking the school calendar. But I'll miss other aspects of having a kid in school. I'll miss the sense of community I've felt while comparing notes with other parents; I'll miss all the Mother's Club meetings and school conferences. And I'll miss the incomparable satisfaction I get every time I work on projects for young people.

This hit me on the long ride home from the campus of the University of Notre Dame, which I toured earlier this month with Nate and three of his closest friends—Andrea, Lauren, and Ryan. Though I've known these kids since they were small, it had been a while since we'd spent so much quality time in my compact station wagon. Between long stretches of road construction, periodic rain showers, and the Bare Naked Ladies blaring on the CD player, I remembered how much I've enjoyed the easy laughter and awesome energy of these kids. And I'm excited about this next phase of their lives.

But whether they head for Notre Dame or Michigan State next fall, I'm going to miss them.

As we drove closer to home, my backseat crew quieted down. The sky cleared, and one of the richest sunsets I'd ever seen suddenly appeared in my rearview mirror. My right foot instinctively moved toward the brake pedal—as if that would make it last a while longer. I didn't notice the cars tailing me on the expressway until Nate pointed out that I was driving like an old woman, way below the speed limit.

Just one more year. Pour it slowly, please.

———————

Class Reunion

June 18, 1994

These days, almost everyone I know is talking about high-school reunions. Conversations typically wander between the topics of weight-loss programs and banquet halls. And suddenly, people we haven't thought of in years rise up to haunt us from the yellowing pages of our yearbooks.

"Is Cathy's ex flying in from Houston?"

"Is Robert bringing his new wife?"

"Should I wear something with sequins?"

No matter how mature we think we are, reunion anxiety lingers like the clammy anticipation of a blind date, right up until the big night rolls around.

But two years ago, less than a month before my own twentieth high-school reunion, my father fell to a fatal heart attack in his driveway. The excitement of the approaching reunion paled in the shadow of Dad's funeral, and the idea of celebrating my high-school years at a gala reception seemed frivolous, almost disrespectful.

"I'm not sure if I can handle this," I told my husband, a fellow graduate of the class of 1972 and my date for the landmark event. I worried that old friends would ask about my father and that I would fall apart. Nonetheless, I agreed to attend, having purchased expensive tickets and offered a ride to another couple several weeks earlier.

An hour and a half before the reunion, I methodically reached into my closet for the simple black dress that had seen me through several semi-formal occasions. I rummaged through my jewelry box to uncover a small strand of pearls, a gift from my parents to commemorate a landmark birthday. I washed my hair and styled it just as I would have on any other Saturday evening.

Driving with my husband and our friends to the reunion, I realized that I had finally crossed the threshold of real adulthood. Unlike our senior prom, the reunion hadn't triggered a moment of angst over what to wear.

But just as I had done at high-school dances, once I arrived I found myself observing my classmates from a distance, still feeling like an observer from another planet. Little had changed. Or rather, time hadn't left visible scratches on anyone. I noticed only the minor surface alterations—graying temples and a few extra pounds discreetly rearranged under sequins or tailored lapels. The class fashion model, now a homemaker, wore less make-up but looked just as elegant and remote as she did at eighteen. The homecoming queens and kings held court on the sidelines of the dance floor; many had become executive assistants and manufacturers' representatives. I assumed they owned the sleek sedans and convertibles parked in front of the banquet hall.

A former classmate approached and embraced me tightly—way too tightly for someone I barely knew at seventeen. I could hear the hollow cracking of my composure, which I had tried so hard to maintain that evening. Meanwhile, other characters from my past whirled around me like the tiny lights spinning from the mirrored ball in the center of the room. Perfume and aftershave mingled with the heady scent of chardonnay and vodka tonics.

"Cindeeeee!! You're still the same—like tenth grade!" someone else chirped. Had the woman remembered me at all, she would have realized that the very bones in my thirty-eight-year-old face had changed, not to mention the deepening shadows under my eyes. Other conversations were lost in the throbbing beat of Bee Gees' disco tunes.

That night, I didn't feel like dancing.

Like my peers, I studied grief and loss much later—years after graduating high school. Since then, I've looked long and hard to find the courage to take life by the arm and wade through its darker passages, and I've forged my strongest bonds with others who've held up a candle along the way. I wasn't able to explain this to a roomful of people I hadn't seen in twenty years. Or perhaps I'd finally outgrown large parties.

Reflecting on my self-conscious youth, I can honestly say I rarely miss it. I don't want to forget the roar of high-school football games or the applause on opening night of the senior play. (I've saved the awards and the playbills.) But those are the dramas of a young girl's past, and I am not the person I was then.

My high-school memories belong in my yearbook. I doubt that I'll dress them up and take them out for another reunion.

Turning Fifty

August 8, 2004

Old birds are hard to pluck.

—German proverb

There's no denying that fifty is a landmark birthday. A turning point. The Big One.

Over the past few months I've been paying close attention to the mirror in my bathroom. Reading my face like a road map, I scrutinize my eyelids and check the skin around my cheekbones. I notice a couple of age spots that can't quite pass as freckles, and my jaw line isn't as sharp as it used to be.

Even my hands are starting to look like a topographical survey. The pale blue veins over my knuckles are more prominent now, and the skin is etched with fine lines and small valleys. But I'm really OK with all of this.

Just before my birthday last week, I remembered the lyrics from "Miles from Nowhere," an old Cat Stevens song I loved when I was in high school:

Lord, my body, it's been a good friend,
But I won't need it when I reach the end.

After all these years, my body has been a very good friend. It has endured years of ballet and highland dancing classes. Its knees were skinned and bruised countless times. Its tonsils were removed; it was hit by a car; it gave birth to one spectacular child. It survived a couple of blood transfusions and two complete hip replacements. And despite the injuries, it managed to travel all over the United States and parts of Europe. I marvel at how my body still works, and I'm forever grateful that it does.

Age spots aside, what I notice most about turning fifty is that I've become more philosophical, less hurried. I care more about things that matter in the long run—deep relationships; good health. I'm not as influenced by the trendy or the superficial. I watch a lot less television and read whatever intrigues me, usually preferring books that never make the best-seller lists.

Lately, too, I've been wearing clothes that work for me, not necessarily what's promoted in fashion magazines. And I don't need to ask anyone if I've made the right choices. I've finally begun to trust my own opinions.

In years to come, I'd like to make a real difference in my community, my world, but accolades and celebrity no longer interest or impress me.

Before taking on any new assignments or volunteer work, I pause to examine my motivations. I want to give from the heart, not the ego. To borrow from Thoreau, I want to live deliberately. Or, as I remind my teen-ager whenever I embarrass him: The older I get, the less I worry about what other people think.

Daily Tribune colleague Kathy Hutson tells me it's very important to have younger friends as you age, "because you'll want to have visitors when you're in the old folks' home." This is great advice. But I also believe that *older* friends help you navigate the thornier parts of middle age, including the empty nest and suspicious mammograms. Like senior discounts and a good eye cream, mature role models are definitely worth seeking out.

A good friend who turned fifty last year has held up a light for me every step of the way, insisting that the fifties can be wild and juicy years if you get your priorities straight. I love her attitude.

"I quit being a doormat and I don't try to please everyone," she says. "I know who I am now."

Isn't it a shame that we have to travel through five decades to figure this out?

———————————

The Wrinkle Wars

April 25, 2004

"This is what 40 looks like. We've been lying so long,
who would know?" —Gloria Steinem

As part of a skincare campaign, the Olay company recently sent me a t-shirt that proclaims: "Love the skin you're in." The promotion works, because I can't get the catchphrase out of my mind.

My girlfriends and I have decided that drugstore creams, including Oil of Olay, work about as well as pricier anti-aging potions sold in better department stores. And we should know. We've tried them all.

None of us are superficial women. We have college degrees, families, and careers we enjoy. But we're still not sure what to make of the changing faces in our mirrors, so we keep on searching for the elixir that guarantees its promise of eternal youth.

More than any generation, baby boomers loathe the idea of growing up. Like edgy toddlers strapped in strollers, we're kicking and screaming all the way to the AARP. I think we could use some mature role models.

I even read somewhere that boomers don't even want to be called Grandma or Grandpa. Those monikers sound stodgy, like the matrons of the 1950s who wore their nylons rolled around their knees. Boomer grandparents wear sweats and have adopted alternative nicknames like Doodum and Mooma. How silly is that?

To my ear, the word grandmother sounds beautiful and comforting. It has a ring of grace and dignity. But I think it's the dignity part that we boomers are struggling with. No matter how far we've traveled, aging is still regarded as our final frontier. A cruel adversary to be conquered at any cost.

Ironically, advertising copywriters keep telling us we're not getting older; we're getting better. Yet we can't visit a drug store or a cosmetic counter without being reminded that our faces and bodies need to be altered, repaired, firmed, smoothed, exfoliated, or lifted entirely. There are endless beauty aisles stocked with fruit acids and other magic formulas to dissolve our encroaching wrinkles and telltale age spots. Mature women—if we're to believe what we read in our magazines—are seriously damaged and need to be fixed.

And consider the middle-aged fashion models whose careers have been resuscitated to appease aging fashionistas. They barely look a day over thirty-five. The message to women is that it really doesn't matter what we've achieved through education, experience, or sheer perseverance. She who looks youngest wins.

My husband tells me that men have aging angst too, although cosmetic issues don't boggle them quite so much. Doug is cool about losing his hair and leaving what's left in its striking shade of gray. As a nod to midlife freedom, he's grown a beard. I think he looks terrific and, yes, dignified.

Men seem more comfortable with "dignified" and I suspect it's because we give them full permission to ripen. We don't marginalize older men the way we marginalize older women. Most men get on with the natural process of aging—and a few of them seize the real privileges of maturity.

Paul Newman's weathered face, for example, recently graced the cover of a business magazine. It stopped me in my tracks. I was immediately struck by the power, depth, and wisdom reflected in those famous blue eyes. Age *is* elegance when it's allowed to tell its own truth.

Years ago, as a college student, I worked at the cosmetics counter of an upscale department store. I'll never forget a customer in her late fifties (I'll call her Mrs. Smith) who haunted our counters weekly for the ultimate anti-aging cream. In my mind, she remains an eerie icon of the woman I don't want to become.

Married to a wealthy businessman, Mrs. Smith was terrified of aging. She'd had several facelifts but looked like a sad marionette, a caricature of her younger self. Chronically disappointed, she often came in to return the creams that "didn't work."

Ever so tactfully, we all tried to explain that cosmetics could enhance maturing beauty, but they did not have the power to totally reverse the handiwork of Mother Time.

But Mrs. Smith didn't love the skin she was in, and I swear she kept our department in business that year.

———————

Like Daughter, Like Mother

May 10, 2003

L ately I've been spending so much time at William Beaumont
Hospital in Royal Oak that I've started calling it "Billy
Beau's."

I used to think of hospitals as citadels of sickness and emergency, but Beaumont has set the stage for some joyful events and
major turning points in my life. This is where, seventeen years ago,
I gave birth to my only child. And where, barely a year ago, I had
both hips replaced and, thanks to a first-rate team of physical thera-
pists, learned how to walk again.

This time I'm back with my mother, who, ironically, is undergo-
ing tests for her first hip replacement surgery. Unfortunately, her
pre-surgical screening has uncovered other health problems, all of
which seem to require another series of medical appointments. But
Mom hasn't lost her wicked sense of humor—one of the many things
I admire about her. Waiting for a CT scan, she laughs between gulps

of the barium "milkshake" she's just been served for the procedure. "Wanna try it?" she quips, waving the shake under my nose. Watching her sip the ghastly white goo from a straw, I laugh along with her, though I know she's had nothing else to eat all day.

A nurse appears in the doorway and calls my mother's name. I'm told to remain here. Mom reaches for her walker and slowly weaves out of the waiting room. I flinch because I know firsthand the bone-deep pain she fights with each step, yet I'm still shocked at how much mobility she's suddenly lost to arthritis. It was only last year when she loaned her bedroom to me and assisted my recovery from the same hip surgery she'll be having in two weeks.

An hour drags on.

Bored with *People* magazine, I close my eyes and try to recall how my mother looked when she was younger. I conjure an ancient memory of my pediatrician's office—the exotic fish floating in the aquarium; the mandatory racks of Dick and Jane books. I was barely six, and Mom was right there with me, promising that the cheerless nurse bearing a sinister tray of syringes and rubbing alcohol was really there to help me.

These days, it's my turn to reassure Mom, and I have to admit it feels a little strange. A friend who's exactly my age reminds me we're now official members of the Sandwich Generation, the ones called to spread our energy thinly between growing offspring and aging parents. But while it's never easy to watch a parent struggle with illness, I don't mind playing my part in our family medical saga.

Just as my mother and I share a genetic history of arthritis, neither of us has any siblings. Perhaps because of that, our relationship is evolving in ways we'd never imagined. The two of us have learned a lot together—and not just about hip replacement. Over the years we've shopped for china patterns, baby toys, school clothes, dining room furniture, kitchen equipment, medical supplies, and funeral directors.

Doug and I were building new careers and trying to keep house when our son was born. But my mother, thank goodness, was always ready and willing to baby-sit her only grandchild. Though she had no experience raising little boys, she boldly navigated the strange mechanical world of trains, cars, and Legos.

And it seems she'd barely claimed her hard-won status as "Grandma" when my father died, making her a widow and changing the shape of our small family circle.

Erma Bombeck once said that mothers "are not the faceless stereotypes who appear once a year on a greeting card with their virtues set to prose, but women who have been dealt a hand for life and play each card one at a time, the best way they know how."

I'm in my late forties now and Mom is in her seventies, but we're still fine-tuning our roles as parent and child; nurse and patient; best friends. And I think we've become more flexible through all we've been dealt, from health crises to chaotic Christmas dinners.

We've learned how durable women can be.

Still, I wish she would stop apologizing for occupying my time in hospital waiting rooms. I've reminded her of the dozens of times she's driven me to the very same waiting rooms here at Billy Beau's, and of all the good things she's done for our family. I remind her it's my turn to be here for her.

But it's no use. I'm still her kid—and she's not keeping score.

Beach Stones

August 22, 2004

For me, the highlight of vacationing on Lake Michigan is the rare chance to collect my wits and a few beach stones. More adventurous souls will dive into its frigid waves or race motor boats and jet skis, but I'd rather mine the shore for treasures.

Morning is the best time to hunt for beach stones. The water is usually calm, your outlook is refreshed, and, if you're really lucky, fellow beachcombers are still asleep. Rising with the sun, you'll get first pick of the gems that rolled in with the tide.

It's always a thrill to uncover exceptional Petoskey stones, which seem to be getting rare these days. But don't overlook the subtle beauty of milky quartz, and keep an eye out for perfect skipping stones that were tumbled smooth by the waves.

Look closely, and you'll find beach stones imprinted with fossils, some bearing an uncanny resemblance to ancient tablets carved with runes or hieroglyphics. Others are miniature works of art—and you'd swear they'd been painted by an Asian calligrapher. As many Northern Michigan jewelers have already discovered, some of these beauties are worthy of stringing on a necklace.

During a recent visit to the Sleeping Bear National Lakeshore, where I celebrated my fiftieth birthday, it occurred to me that collecting beach stones is a bit like crafting a life. You have to remain grounded and focused, yet always open to new possibilities.

For starters, you need deep pockets to collect your bounty. And you must begin your quest believing that you'll be rewarded with more than you bargained for. If you focus solely on the obvious—Petoskey stones, for instance—you might miss the other jewels of the lake. In my search for something rare or perfect, I've nearly overlooked other stones of beauty and character.

And as every seasoned beachcomber knows, the rippling water teases like a mirage, making it hard to see things as they really are. I've rescued many stones that looked tempting under water, but were lackluster when they dried in the sun. Some were merely pieces of beach glass.

Selecting beach stones, in fact, is a bit like choosing what is essential in life: friends, partners, schools, career paths, a church, and a place to call home. It's wise to make these choices slowly and carefully; to consider what feels right, lasting, and true.

As the cliché goes, it's possible to have too much of a good thing, and beach stones are no exception. I always end up with too many, and have to edit my finds down to an exemplary few. Otherwise, I'd need a gravel truck to haul them back to Detroit.

This is a lesson I need to apply at home, too.

I tend to hang on to some things longer than I should—outdated clothes, shoes, grudges, bad ideas, hairstyles, broken tools, receipts, and stale opinions. And over the years I've tolerated things I should have protested, including dumb TV shows, junk food, unfair wages, and degrading articles in women's magazines.

Wandering the shore, I ask myself: What's really essential now?

How much of what I buy do I really need? How can I make better use of my time and the blessings I've been given? Whose script am I living?

Collecting beach stones, I'm reminded that the second half of life offers the freedom to choose again—to polish, edit, refine and reconsider.

Once again, I empty my pockets before returning home.

———————————

Wisdom from the Aging

January 17, 2004

old on to your AARP card! Many influential baby boomers
are turning fifty this year. That list includes Oprah Winfrey,
whose birthday is January 29, not to mention several illus-
trious locals and old friends who made me promise I wouldn't print
their names in a column about aging.

So I asked a few whose wit and wisdom I admire—cancer survivors, educators, publishers, attorneys, retired executives, and empty
nesters—to anonymously share their advice on how to grow up gracefully. Their precepts also make terrific resolutions for the New Year,
no matter how old you are. Here's what our local sages had to say:

1. Be yourself. The greatest gift of maturity is uncovering who
   you really are. Life gets more interesting (and so do you)
   when you stop worrying about what other people think. Go
   ahead and wear what you like. Paint your office red. Take up
   the kazoo.

2. No matter how long you've put it off, learn how to iron your own clothes.

3. Botox and facelifts won't fix a sagging inner life. Love your laugh lines and get over your bald spot.

4. Practice generosity because it makes you beautiful. Be the first to pick up the check in restaurants. Pay compliments. Give up grudges.

5. Choose your battles carefully. Nobody can be right all of the time.

6. The lessons we learn from hard times are worth a degree from Harvard. Crisis isn't necessarily a bad word.

7. Stop worshiping celebrities. There are plenty of stellar individuals to admire in your neighborhood, and they're probably not in legal trouble.

8. Be worthy of admiration, especially to young people.

9. Ask stupid questions. How else can you learn?

10. Never stop educating yourself. Read often; visit museums; watch public television.

11. Travel while your joints and bowels still work. See the wonders of this magnificent world.

12. Career success is highly over-rated, but you'll never regret the time you spent with your kids.

13. Never own more of anything than you can fit in a drawer.

14. Nothing ages you faster than spending time with complainers, nit-pickers, and self-appointed victims. Fill your address

book with people who treat you with respect and are fun to be with.

15. Take charge of your health. Don't expect your doctors to be magicians.

16. Never miss a chance to express gratitude to anyone. Count your blessings daily and thank God for all you have. He doesn't require hand-written notes.

17. Find a church and join a faith community you can count on when the sermon is over. Being part of something larger pulls you out of yourself and makes a big difference in your life.

18. Find something you love to do and stick with it.

19. Find someone you love and stick with them.

20. Never take your spouse or loved one for granted. Imagine what life would be like if they were suddenly gone.

21. Stop wearing shoes that hurt.

22. Keep bottled water in the basement. The world is a crazy place.

23. Keep dreaming big, but never underestimate the small victories.

24. Quit saving the good stuff—dishes, clothes, or gifts—for special occasions. Remember that each day is banquet, and refuse to accept only leftovers. Celebrate every day as if it were your last on the planet, because someday it will be.

Soul Caring

Where's Walden?

October 3, 1997

T hanks to the wonders of modern technology, I now have a mind-boggling array of options.

I can shop for birthday gifts on the Internet, watch a funeral in Britain on live television, and order a complete wardrobe from a computer catalog.

A mother who works as a journalist, I also have the option of conducting my business in an office building or working at home on my computer while caring for my child. (In ten years I could be wearing my computer on a string around my neck, or so the folks at the Massachusetts Institute of Technology tell me.)

Every day I have more choices than I can reasonably consider. And so, like other tired Americans, I carry the burden of complexity—a burden so overwhelming, in fact, that there are times when I imagine trading places with Henry David Thoreau.

It's only fitting that I rediscovered Thoreau the week I purged my home office with a dust rag and a vacuum cleaner. The autumn mornings felt ripe for pitching and sorting, for creating blank space where none existed before. *Walden,* Thoreau's famous treatise on simple living, was jammed behind a pile of unread paperbacks on an overcrowded shelf.

Like other writers with good intentions, I've admired Thoreau but hadn't read *Walden* since it appeared many years ago on a required reading list at my state university. I'd retained only a few pithy quotes, and recalled only sketchy details of Thoreau's spartan cabin in the woods of Concord, Massachusetts. But suddenly, here was the book, whispering to me across the century —"Simplify, simplify"—and begging me to take another look.

Glancing through the pages, I realized Thoreau's words had been wasted on me when I first read them. At the time I was a young college student living in a cramped dormitory, eager to graduate and buy enough furniture to fill a spacious suburban apartment.

"Most of the luxuries, and many of the so-called comforts of life, are not only not indispensable, but positive hindrances to the elevation of mankind," Thoreau warned in the chapter titled "Economy." Only an overworked adult—one who is drowning in the debris of modern life and pressed by the weight of too many commitments—could truly appreciate Thoreau's genius, I mused as I kept reading.

Yet it also occurred to me that things were vastly different for Thoreau. The "comforts of life" in the 1840s were not exactly cushy by today's standards. His concept of luxury might have been taking tea in his mother's bone china saucers. So what had he given up to commune with nature?

Even before he moved to Walden Pond, Thoreau hadn't accumulated three television sets or a closetful of designer clothes. He didn't own several pairs of expensive athletic shoes for all those philosophical walks he took. He didn't wonder where he'd store his blender or Tupperware while he roughed it in the woods. His cot in the cabin couldn't have been lumpier than the straw-filled mattresses in most mid-nineteenth-century homes. And Thoreau never had to trade a personal computer for a pencil.

With all due respect, I wonder, how tough was Thoreau's sabbatical with simplicity? Is it true that he occasionally walked from Walden Pond back to Concord, where Emerson's wife had a home-cooked supper waiting for him?

As Andrew Delbanco notes in his wise book, *Required Reading: Why Our American Classics Matter Now* (Farrar, Straus and Giroux), reading Thoreau can make us feel "accused of hoarding comforts." We might even try to find holes in Thoreau's impassioned pitch for the simple life.

And yet Thoreau is, as Delbanco says, "an irresistible writer; to read him is to feel wrenched away from the customary world and delivered into a place we fear as much as we need."

How true. Just as Thoreau did, I'd like to weed out, pare down, live deliberately, be a resident philosopher. (Would the family miss me?) A life devoid of clutter sounds positively blissful, especially when there are no empty spaces on my calendar.

But making choices is so much more difficult in a culture fueled by sheer busyness and commercialism. There are few places, few wooded Waldens, where one can escape the incessant bombardment of to-do lists or product advertising.

Visiting the "real" Walden Pond in Concord for the first time this fall, I was amazed and disappointed to find the place overrun. Locals were strewn on its small beach. You couldn't walk the path around the pond without rubbing shoulders with other curious sightseers; there wasn't a spot left for solitary reflection.

If nothing else, my rendezvous with Thoreau got me thinking. What—and how much—do I really need? What price have I paid for modern technology and convenience? In which landfill will all my stuff end up?

And how would I fare if I were delivered into a place I fear as much as I need, as Delbanco put it? Could I survive in a one-room cabin with barely more than a chair, a wooden table, a bowlful of raw vegetables, and my laptop? Honestly, I wish I could.

Biopsy

January 2, 2000

_____

Even the most painful biopsy has a silver lining and several lessons to teach.

When my breast surgeon called last week with the good news—no malignancy found—I felt like Ebenezer Scrooge after the Ghost of Christmas Future sent him skipping down the path of redemption. A shroud was lifted, and my other Christmas gifts paled in comparison. If you've ever endured a similar experience, especially during the holiday season, you know exactly what I mean.

Waiting for the results of any medical test can seem like eternity. And when you're suspended in biopsy limbo, the texture of daily life feels as sheer and fragile as gauze.

It helps to have network of support. During the week-long stretch between the hospital visit and the surgeon's phone call, I received many soothing e-mails and hand-written notes from people who understood I was in a holding pattern and not quite in the mood for Christmas. They knew I was scared and stuck, even when I insisted I was doing just fine, thank you. And nobody pointed out how horribly self-preoccupied I was.

Biopsies remind us how important it is to hang up our pride and say exactly what we mean. We remember how soothing it feels to hear dear ones say "I love you," and how empowering it is to return those three words with a full heart.

"If you need to talk or cry, I'm here!" wrote a breast cancer survivor who had endured much more than a biopsy. My mother brought me a bouquet of spring flowers precisely at the moment I needed to see something other than holiday greens. My husband hugged me often.

I was also surprised at the newfound ease with which my friends and I discussed topics usually reserved for church. We launched many conversations about the emotional earthquake that rumbles when our annual medical check-ups reveal that our bodies aren't immortal after all.

Religious denominations blurred, too. Readers from several different churches told me they added my name to prayer circles and prayer lists. And during the surgical procedure, I had kept in my back pocket a holy card of St. Therese of Lisieux, which was given to me earlier that week by a couple of Catholic friends.

How could I possibly doubt the healing, unifying power of prayer and friendship?

A health crisis of any kind can turn everything upside down. A surgeon told me it's not uncommon for biopsy patients to reorder their priorities while awaiting results. Their former problems seem less significant, and ordinary life suddenly shimmers like newly fallen snow.

Of course, as the weeks pass and things return to normal, we tend to forget. We lose our liberating perspective. Our cats start pooping on the Oriental rugs again, and the Visa bills roll in like carloads of annoying relatives on Christmas Eve.

But wouldn't it be wonderful to retain the spiritual lessons from a biopsy—long after the scars and bruises heal, and it's back to business as usual?

Hope Is a Thing with Feathers

March 5, 2000

O ur friend George recently announced that his mother-in-law
just celebrated her ninety-sixth birthday. This "inspiring
woman," as George describes her, also renewed her subscrip-
tion to *Reminisce*, her favorite magazine, for another three years.

"Three years," George repeated, smiling. "That's what I call real
optimism. I suppose everyone needs something to look forward to."

Call it optimism or hope, the anticipation of pleasure keeps us
moving toward an uncertain future, even if the odds seem stacked
against us. This is why we bother to plant spring bulbs in autumn
when our gardens look ragged and the earth is chilling out. And it's
why we plant maple seedlings on the front lawn, even if we suspect
we won't be around to see them reach their optimal height.

But it's hard to keep the faith sometimes, especially during the
first half of March, which has to be the soggiest, most depressing
time of the year in Michigan. As Carl Sandburg noted, "In times like

these, you have to be an optimist to open your eyes when you wake in the morning."

Spring isn't far away, officially, though it doesn't help to remember the fact when you're staring out your office window at a monochromatic landscape and it occurs to you that your next-door neighbors are swilling margaritas right now in Cancun. Or when you turn on the news and hear the latest reports on Middle East conflicts and local high-school bomb threats.

Or when one of your former college roommates sends an e-mail message explaining how the body of a sixteen-year-old girl from her neighborhood was found in a ditch, six bullets in the back of her head, after disappearing from her job at the local Taco Bell. Reading Libby's description of this drug-related murder in her "sheltered little town" in Virginia was like swallowing an ice cube whole. I also worried about Libby's own teen-aged daughters, who were devastated by the news when it was announced at their school.

"Life can be a crapshoot, and I doubt that our children are ever really safe. Sorry to sound so depressing, but you caught me on a horrible day," Libby concluded in her e-mail. "On top of this tragedy, I have the end-of-the-winter blues. Do you think spring is really coming this year?"

That particular afternoon, I wasn't so sure. Libby's e-mail reawakened in me the primordial fear that all mothers try to put back to sleep. When catastrophe strikes children, it is hard not to feel sad and angry and utterly powerless. The only thing I could think of to tell my friend was that I believe the first step in transforming a violent world is to try to be better parents to our own kids. And we must never, ever stop believing in the possibility of a brighter, peaceful future.

Kent Nerburn, author of *Small Graces*, writes: "Though we may not live a holy life, we live in a world alive with holy moments. We need only take the time to bring these moments into light."

Rinsing dishes last week, I noticed that the cactus on the window ledge above the sink had finally produced its first bloom. Nate had given this plant to me several years ago for Mother's Day, back when he was a foot shorter and still in grade school. The pot in which it was presented is hand-painted in the giddy primary colors of childhood, with the words "Happy Mom's Day" printed boldly inside a slightly lopsided heart. It has been a fixture in the window for so long that I usually look right past it.

But the sudden appearance of the cactus bloom—a riotous, neon-pink blossom dangling from its leggy stem like a jazzy earring—made me see it with new eyes. You'd have thought I'd just discovered a forgotten twenty dollar bill in a coat pocket.

"Wow, take a look at this," I shouted, dragging Nate to the window for a closer look at the cactus. Despite his cool teen-aged self, my boy flashed a quick smile, amused that such a small gift from a long-ago holiday could resurrect his loony mother's entire afternoon.

Courage in Our Pockets

June 13, 2004

A gift is as a precious stone in the eyes of the one who has it.
—Proverbs

It was one of those simple gestures you remember for years. I was sifting through the day's mail, three years ago, just a week before I was scheduled for major surgery. Hidden between the bills and catalogs was a small envelope from Miner's Den, a Royal Oak business I've patronized for many years.

Expecting an ad for a jewelry sale, I was surprised to find a personal greeting card with a guardian angel coin inside. Also included was a short poem titled "Angel in My Pocket," which explained, in so many words, that I could count on my guardian angel to keep me company during the surgical ordeal I was preparing for.

The card was signed, "From your friends at Miner's Den," and it couldn't have arrived at a better time.

I had been trying hard to appear optimistic for my family and friends, but was secretly terrified of the hip replacement surgery ahead. The folks at Miner's Den had seen me hobbling around their store on a cane earlier that week, so they must have sensed that I needed to remember the very real presence of guardian angels. That little coin traveled in my suitcase to the hospital, by the way, and someday I'll pass it along to someone else who needs an angel.

We all need something that feels comforting to the touch, whether it's a special coin, a smooth river stone, or a set of prayer beads. Belief in mystical powers isn't required. These icons mainly serve to remind us we're not alone in our struggles.

Several years ago, when my friend Debbie and I were shopping together, we noticed a display of "spirit stones" in a local gift shop. Each of these small stones was etched with a Native American symbol and polished to a soft sheen. Debbie was going through an especially rough time, and was drawn to the stone depicting a bear claw. It represented "courage," so I bought it for her on the spot.

I'd completely forgotten about the courage stone until last month, when Debbie and I were participating in a women's retreat with our church group. The theme was inspired by the National Day of Prayer, which coincided neatly with the first day of our retreat.

During our evening discussion in the retreat center's library, Nora, another member of our group, asked us all to pray for the courage she needed to help mend an injured friendship. A moment of silence passed. Then, after taking something from her purse, Debbie rose from her seat and walked toward Nora.

As Debbie opened her hand, I saw the courage stone I'd given her years ago.

"It's time for me to pass a little courage on to someone else," Debbie told Nora, explaining how the stone had been given to her when she needed it. "Keep this with you when you need support."

I was almost as surprised and touched as Nora was.

"It was a gift of immeasurable value, for many reasons," Nora told me later. "The stone isn't just about courage, it's about friendship. I'll definitely pass it along to someone else when the time is right."

It's easy to get caught up in the economic pressures of gift-giving, especially during the summer months, when many of us have more weddings, showers, and graduation parties than we can easily manage.

Still, I'm convinced that the gifts we treasure most are the small, unexpected ones that show someone was paying attention to our needs and challenges.

And when you consider their tremendous ripple effect, tokens like the guardian angel coin and the courage stone are so much larger than they appear.

Mrs. Lindbergh's Gift

February 18, 2001

"Did you know Anne Morrow Lindbergh died yesterday?" Doug asked, thumbing through a stack of newspapers I hadn't read.

The half-page obituary for Mrs. Lindbergh caught his attention because he remembered she was the author of *Gift from the Sea*, a little book I've kept for years on my nightstand and treasure so much that I own three yellowed copies of its first edition.

Though I'm not one to shed tears over celebrity obits, Mrs. Lindbergh's was a stirring tribute to an old friend—a cherished friend and mentor who will never know how many hours of comfort and reassurance she's given me.

She was ninety-four when she died February 7 in her rural Vermont home. For many Americans, she was best known as the wife of aviator Charles Lindbergh. The two flew together in a plane on their first date, later becoming famous as the pioneering couple who flew across oceans and around the world. Never out of the public eye, the Lindberghs were the center of worldwide attention again in 1932 when their firstborn, Charles Jr., was kidnapped and later found dead.

But it was Mrs. Lindbergh's career as a writer that really intrigued me.

After Charles Jr., she raised five other children in the Lindbergh limelight. Yet somehow she managed to publish thirteen books of essays, letters and diaries chronicling her intricately organized life as a record-setting aviator, wife, and mother. How she managed to juggle these myriad roles always seemed a remarkable feat to me, especially since I struggle daily to find time to write newspaper columns while raising only one child.

For years, Mrs. Lindbergh's book of reflections, *Gift from the Sea* (Pantheon), has provided the guidance I've needed to help balance my marriage and family; work and rest.

Written during a brief ocean-side sabbatical, *Gift from the Sea* was first published in 1955. The slim volume spoke to women on the brink of social change—women who were primarily responsible for raising families and conflicted by the new career opportunities opening up to them. Years ahead of its time, it soon became a classic among inspirational best-sellers, yet its success always baffled its author.

"The original astonishment remains…that a book of essays, written to work out my own problems, should have spoken to so many other women," Lindbergh admitted twenty years after *Gift* was published.

A wise friend of mine recommended the book when I was in my early thirties, when everything in my small universe was spinning faster than I could keep up. I was raising a preschooler. Working as a travel magazine editor. Striving to be a community activist. And all the while attempting to make a home out of a handyman special.

As much as I'd welcomed so many options, I was too exhausted to understand why I always felt something was still missing.

Mrs. Lindbergh knew exactly how to explain my dilemma.

"There are so few empty pages in my engagement calendar…Too many worthy activities, valuable things, and interesting people," she wrote in one of her essays. "For it is not merely the trivial which clutters our lives but the important as well. We can have a surfeit of treasures—an excess of shells, where one or two would be significant."

Mrs. Lindbergh knew also that composing a sane and satisfying life isn't simply a matter of reassessing priorities or clearing spaces on a day planner. Decades before Thomas Moore made "soul caring" a household term, Mrs. Lindbergh understood that most American women are starved for a spiritual life. A meaningful life.

The real issue, she wrote, "is how to remain whole in the midst of the distractions of life…It is the spirit of woman that is going dry, not the mechanics that are wanting; certainly our lives are easier, freer, more open to opportunities. But these hard-won prizes are insufficient because we have not yet learned how to use them."

Nearly fifty years later, we're still struggling to solve the same dilemmas. Anne Morrow Lindbergh asserted that women must be the "pioneers" in the movement toward re-creating lives of grace and harmony.

I'm forever grateful to her for illuminating the trail ahead of us, for her *Gift from the Sea.*

Holy Fools and
Juggling Priests

April 18, 2004

"Drop the idea that you are Atlas carrying the world on your shoulders. The world would go on without you. Don't take yourself so seriously."   —Norman Vincent Peale

His name is Mudhead, and I found him on vacation one summer at a Native American art gallery in Wisconsin. Though I don't collect kachina dolls, this little guy had to come home in my suitcase.

According to Hopi legend, Mudhead is the clown of ceremonial dances. His duty as a cosmic trickster is to amuse the audience during pauses in sacred rituals. Leaping around the circle, Mudhead reminds the big chiefs that a higher power is in control and they need to lighten up. He is both ridiculous and humbling—and essential to the dance.

Covered head to toe in feathers and fringe, my little Mudhead kachina now perches on a shelf in my office as a spirited reminder to stop taking myself so seriously. And I need to be reminded often.

It also occurs to me that, until recently, humor hasn't played such a vital part in mainstream religions. During a heartfelt discussion, a friend told me he left the church of his youth because, as he put it, "I got the idea that they didn't want me to enjoy myself."

Guilt and fear, he said, were the overriding emotions he felt every time he attended a service. Moments of joy and pleasure were rarely encouraged, even during holidays. And humor? You've got to be kidding. My friend couldn't imagine the clergy cracking a smile, let alone a joke.

I tactfully suggested that perhaps things are changing. This morning, in fact, many churches around the country are celebrating Holy Fools Sunday, also known as Holy Hilarity Sunday. The festivities, which vary depending on the style and temperament of each congregation, are a modest equivalent to Mudhead's clownish dance around the campfire. Congregants might wear silly hats or sell popcorn in the sanctuary; pastors wear their vestments backwards. This is a good sign.

But childhood wounds run deep, and my friend doesn't plan to revisit his religious past, especially not in the wake of newsworthy church scandals. For spiritual sustenance he'd rather watch Wayne Dyer on public television.

I've witnessed the type of religious leaders my friend has shunned, but I'm hoping they are the exception and no longer the rule. And while I've yet to meet a holy man who owns a Whoopee Cushion, I do know of a priest who juggles.

Our national news media could learn a few lessons from Mudhead, too. Whenever I watch too much television, for instance, I'm convinced that we're all doomed to suffer on a miserable, hopeless planet. From incurable diseases to random violence, there's never a shortage of horrific fodder to fuel my worries and make me think twice before leaving the house. And sometimes, like my friend who left his church, I feel inexplicably guilty when I do let go and enjoy myself.

But not having fun—especially during cynical times—shows a serious lack of faith. I read somewhere that the word "silly" has roots in the Greek term "selig," which means "blessed." In other words, it's probably not a stretch to say that good humor has a spark of the divine.

Political commentator H. L. Mencken loosely defined Puritanism as "the haunting fear that someone, somewhere, may be having a good time." I think Mudhead would agree.

Retreating

---

our times a year, I indulge in a ritual that puzzles my neighbors, not to mention my family.

It goes something like this: I get up early on a weekday and load my car with two tote bags—one crammed with books, the other with pajamas and a toothbrush. I back out of the driveway quickly and disappear for twenty-four hours. The next day, I come back looking as if I'd spent a full week at the spa. My sacred escape, as I call it, is a mere twenty minutes from home, but seems a universe away.

"So, did you have fun at the monastery?" Doug teases when I return.

My hideaway isn't exactly a monastery, but it's the next best thing. Secluded on a wooded estate in Bloomfield Hills, Manresa Jesuit Retreat House remains one of Oakland County's best-kept secrets. It's where I go when my shoulders lock up and I can't shut out the white noise buzzing in my head. It's where I turn when I feel unappreciated, uninspired, and overwhelmed.

No, Manresa doesn't offer facials, pedicures, or therapeutic massages. And while the historic Tudor-revival mansion has opened its meeting facilities to business groups, it remains, at its heart, a place for the spirit. Religious artwork and gilded icons decorate the hallways, while Stations of the Cross and Catholic statuary grace several acres of tranquil garden paths.

And nobody goes home hungry. On a recent overnight retreat, three friends and I enjoyed heaping portions of "Jesuit cuisine"—a divine menu of real comfort food, including roast chicken, green beans, and buttery mashed potatoes. And, as we quickly discovered on previous retreats, there's always a plate of homemade cookies left out in the dining room for snacking.

After dinner, my friends and I usually set aside time alone for reading and reflection. While I often read inspirational literature at home, I enjoy this genre most in the sanctuary of my private room at Manresa. (The paneled library downstairs, in fact, is where I first discovered the writings of Henri J. M. Nouwen.)

Spending just a few hours this way, I feel as if my frazzled parts had been gently polished and reconnected.

I highly recommend retreating to everyone, regardless of religious affiliation. Women, especially, need to give ourselves permission to step aside for a breather, even if our loved ones think we're being unsociable, or, heaven forbid, neglectful. Our devotion to family and career seldom allows time to quench the soul, and few of us have a quiet place where we can pause to refuel.

Unlike health spas, where the lodgings are typically deluxe, religious retreat houses offer minimal amenities. Expect no television and very few distractions. Manresa, for example, enforces periods of silence that must be respected by all guests.

A spiritual retreat can be held in any secluded location, but be sure to plan well in advance. Leave office machines behind and cell phones turned off. And if you're not attending a guided retreat, prepare your own list of activities—group discussions, personal journaling, meditation, or prayer focus.

Wherever you retreat, your aim should be to return to your daily responsibilities with fresh perspective and a renewed spirit to share with others.

In Praise of Shining

September 1999

---

*"One can never consent to creep when one feels
an impulse to soar."*   —Helen Keller

P edaling my bike through our suburb on a bright August afternoon, I noticed two little girls walking hand-in-hand on the sidewalk. Both were wearing party dresses in riotous shades of pink and purple. The taller of the two also sported a large gold crown studded with a galaxy of artificial gemstones.

What really impressed me, though, was the way the crowned princess carried herself ("strutted" would be a better word) and how her towheaded companion bounced alongside as if there were nothing unusual about having a friend who wears a crown on a stroll through the neighborhood. I almost laughed aloud at the notion of doing something equally audacious with one of my middle-aged walking pals. At our age, we do everything we can to preserve our graying dignity.

But very young children rarely hesitate to shine. Most are born with a natural grasp of the Biblical paraphrase, "Don't hide your light under a bushel."

So when does our God-given enthusiasm start to dim? Why, as we mature, do we worry that we'll be out of place if we speak out, or that maybe we're a little too glittery for our own good? Why do we often hesitate to share our unique gifts with the rest of our world? It could be, as Marianne Williamson explains in *A Return to Love* (HarperCollins), that "our deepest fear is not that we are inadequate. Our deepest fear is that we are powerful beyond measure."

Young girls of my vintage received mixed messages growing up. While some of us were encouraged to make the most of our talents, we were often reminded that it's rude to show off.

I remember times in my early teens when classmates won special honors—crowns or trophies—that I'd hoped to win. Witnessing their victories, I suffered a confusing mix of emotions from wounded pride to pea-green envy. Ironically, I also remember feeling apologetic for my own accomplishments, no matter how hard I'd worked for them. Somehow, I'd swallowed the misconception that there were only so many accolades to go around, and it was selfish to grab more than one's share.

I also had several girlfriends who traded academic achievement for popularity. It was, in those days, risky to do anything that set you too far above the pack or made you look smarter than the boys. Too many of us settled for mediocrity. Terrified of our own inner light, even the most capable among us chose to be spectators in the back row, always conforming, never attracting too much attention.

Young girls today seem to have the confidence to unleash their personal power, but they still need our voices in the cheering section.

If a young woman wants to fully embrace her innate worth, how and where does she begin, asks Judith Couchman in *Designing A Woman's Life* (Multnomah Books). "It seems a long jump over the chasm between our gnawing uncertainties and such lavish self-esteem."

Yes, it is a long jump. But as Couchman wisely reminds us, everyone around us will benefit when we leap for our highest goals and finally make it to the other side of the chasm.

The little girl who strutted through my suburb in her crown seemed to know this instinctively. She didn't need special permission to shine, nor did her friend appear to resent her radiance. I'm guessing the two were on their way home to change costumes, secure in the knowledge that they could be anything they imagined.

Being Still

April 4, 2004

One of my favorite traditions at First Congregational Church of Royal Oak is the silent meditation service we hold in the spring, usually before Easter. Sometimes an organist provides soulful background music, and occasionally we do short readings between longer periods of silence.

The midweek candlelit service is led by church members, and this year it's my turn to help open it. We offer this service during Lent because it is, as T.S. Eliot wrote, "a time of tension between dying and rebirth." It is the perfect opportunity for reflection; a time to meditate on the fearsome darkness of the tomb and the pending miracle of Easter.

While a silent service is simple enough to plan, it isn't as easy to carry out. Few of us are comfortable "being still" in a sanctuary with other people sitting near us. We expect to be enlightened, educated, entertained, preached to, or otherwise distracted from the white noise in our heads. Meditation makes us fidgety.

As Sue Monk Kidd notes in her memoir, *When the Heart Waits* (Harper & Row), one of the guiding principles of American culture is "All lines must keep moving." Even when we're home alone, we rush to fill the void with mindless activity or television. Kidd says we resist getting quiet because we're afraid to confront our own darkness.

Yet real miracles occur during moments of being still—and waiting in the dark. Spring bulbs do their hardest labor underground before blooming. Likewise, the work of spiritual growth and healing is done in silence. The time I woke up alone in a dark hospital room, two years ago, immediately comes to mind.

It was just past midnight, a few hours after my second hip surgery. Barely conscious, I awoke to discover my legs were strapped to a large foam wedge to keep me from moving. While I realized this was essential to my recovery, I still felt trapped and terrified. Equally scary was the sensation of waking up alone in a strange room. (I didn't recall being wheeled in after surgery, of course.) And while most hospitals are buzzing with activity during the day and evening, the earliest hours of the morning are eerily quiet.

Breaking the silence, I shouted for help and pushed every button within reach. It was the first time I'd experienced a full-blown panic attack.

When my nurse arrived, she explained that my panic was probably triggered by withdrawal from the anesthesia. She promised to check back periodically. Meanwhile, I kept a light on above my bed. Afraid to fall asleep, I prayed every prayer I could remember and kept vigil for daybreak.

By the time the sun rose, I'd finally calmed down and accepted my temporary state of immobility. And in a luminous moment of grace, I suddenly knew I'd been given a second chance. I knew that I *would* heal and walk again. It would take time, but everything would be okay. And it was. Three days later, I was released early from the hospital to recover in bed at home.

A week before that last surgery, my friend Jenny had sent me a note of encouragement, which included a quote by Patrick Overton. Here's how it begins:

> When you come to the edge of all the light you have and must take a step into the darkness of the unknown, believe that one of two things will happen to you: Either there will be something solid for you to stand on, or, you will be taught how to fly.

I've posted that quote where I can see it on my desk every day. It's the one I like to remember when I'm stumbling in the dark or feeling stuck—or waiting impatiently for a new season to begin.

————————

The Altar in My Kitchen Window

September 20, 2004

"Be faithful in small things because it is in them that your strength lies." —Mother Teresa

Even people who aren't particularly religious or superstitious will admit to owning a talisman of some sort, whether it's a lucky charm on a keychain or a holy card.

My mother recently handed Nate a bronze guardian angel pin that had been given to her by a friend prior to major surgery. "Keep this in your pocket or in the car," she instructed her grandson. "You'll need it a lot more than I do, what with all your driving to and from college."

Another friend, who isn't particularly devout, won't set foot on an airplane without a St. Christopher medal.

Regardless of spiritual practice or religious affiliation, many of us also create shrines and altars using ordinary objects—although we're not always conscious of doing so. Checking several dictionaries, I found the word "shrine" defined as a container for sacred relics; a holy place of worship; the tomb of a holy person; and a niche or alcove for displaying icons. The fifth definition in the *Encarta Dictionary* is my favorite, describing a shrine as "something revered," which can mean any special object or a place that we honor for its unique associations or history.

Your own shrine might be a gallery of preschool drawings and baby pictures held in place with magnets on the refrigerator.

Or maybe it's a piano-top display of sepia-toned photographs of your ancestors.

Or a perennial garden planted in memory of a beloved pet.

Or a small velvet-lined box containing the anniversary watch and cufflinks your father once wore.

Along the same lines, the scrapbooks we craft from old greeting cards and restaurant menus are also holy books venerating the people and events we want to remember. And every time we set the dinner table with heirloom china and candles, we're creating an altar that elevates the family meal to an act of reverence.

My kitchen windowsill has become a small shrine of sorts, although I hadn't planned it that way initially. It began with a few gifts and trinkets I had nowhere else to display, and over the years the assembly just kept growing.

This is where I keep all the Virgin Mary dashboard ornaments I've rescued from local garage sales. And guarding the row of Blessed Mothers is a miniature Mr. Potato Head, complete with spare parts, which once served as a reminder to keep my sense of humor during two joint-replacement surgeries I had three years ago. Mr. Potato Head also keeps company with a tiny Buddha figurine, a gift chosen specifically to remind me to sit still and savor the present moment. At the other end of the window stands a small wooden bear picked up on a family vacation in Northern Michigan.

The anchor of the whole collection is a colorful flower pot embellished with the words "HAPPY MOM'S DAY," which Nate

294

painted ages ago when he was in grade school. Near it I've placed a small statue of St. Francis of Assisi, arms joyously outstretched, purchased on a recent visit to the University of Notre Dame, where Nate began his freshman year last month.

Tucked amid the collection is an old thank-you note sent by a couple of friends after a memorable dinner party. The sentiment on the front of the card neatly sums up the philosophy that gets me through the longest day: "The sacred is in the ordinary. It is found in one's daily life—in friends, family, and neighbors; in one's own backyard."

Ironically, I used to spend a fair amount of time scheming and struggling to earn what others would consider greater things in the world outside. There are few awards, accolades, or gold stars for those of us who work at home. But the longer I live, the only thing I know for certain is this: Everything I hold sacred is hidden right here in plain sight.

Whether I'm at the kitchen window doing dishes or preparing a meal, I notice my icons of the ordinary and give thanks.

To contact the author, please send e-mail to cindy@laferle.com

or visit Cindy's Home Office at www.laferle.com